Britain's Preserved Railways

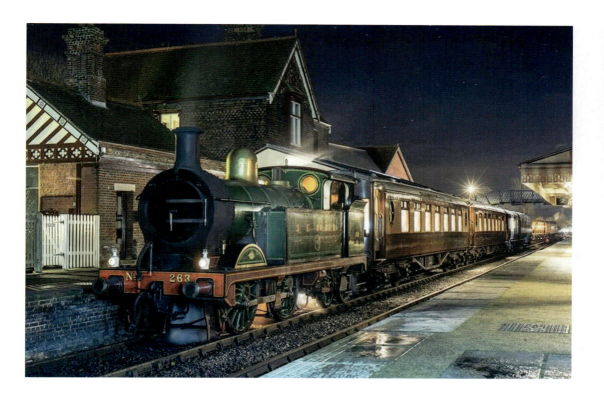

ANDY FLOWERS

Key Books

Front cover: On 31 August 2018, GWR 5101 Class 2-6-2T 5199 departs from the picturesque Berwyn Station on the Llangollen Railway on a service to Llangollen, with the Chain Bridge over the River Dee in the background.

Back cover: 20227 at North Weald (Epping Ongar Railway) on 9 October 2021 with a service for Ongar.

Contents page: 50035 at Bridgnorth (Severn Valley Railway) on 29 December 2021 with a service for Kidderminster.

Published by Key Books
An imprint of Key Publishing Ltd
PO Box 100
Stamford
Lincs PE19 1XQ

www.keypublishing.com

The right of Andy Flowers to be identified as the author of this book has been asserted in accordance with the Copyright, Designs and Patents Act 1988 Sections 77 and 78.

Copyright © Andy Flowers, 2022

ISBN 978 1 80282 210 6

All rights reserved. Reproduction in whole or in part in any form whatsoever or by any means is strictly prohibited without the prior permission of the Publisher.

Typeset by SJmagic DESIGN SERVICES, India.

Contents

Introduction 5
Chapter 1   **South West** 6
    Avon Valley Railway 6
    Bodmin & Wenford Railway 9
    Dartmouth Steam Railway 11
    Dean Forest Railway 14
    East Somerset Railway 17
    Gloucestershire Warwickshire Steam Railway 19
    South Devon Railway 22
    Swanage Railway 25
    Swindon & Cricklade Railway 28
    West Somerset Railway 30
Chapter 2   **South East** 33
    Bluebell Railway 33
    Chinnor & Princes Risborough Railway 36
    Cholsey & Wallingford Railway 38
    Didcot Railway Centre 40
    Kent and East Sussex Railway 43
    Spa Valley Railway 46
    Watercress Line/Mid-Hants Railway 49
Chapter 3   **East of England** 52
    Colne Valley Railway 52
    Epping Ongar Railway 54
    Mid-Norfolk Railway 57
    Nene Valley Railway 60
    North Norfolk Railway 62
Chapter 4   **East Midlands** 65
    Barrow Hill Roundhouse 65
    Battlefield Line 67
    Ecclesbourne Valley Railway 70
    Great Central Railway 73
    Midland Railway – Butterley 77
    Northampton & Lamport Railway 81
    Nottingham Heritage Railway 82
    Peak Rail 85

Chapter 5	**West Midlands**	89
	Chasewater Railway	89
	Churnet Valley Railway	91
	Severn Valley Railway	93
	Statfold Barn	96
Chapter 6	**Yorkshire**	100
	Embsay & Bolton Abbey Steam Railway	100
	Keighley & Worth Valley Railway	103
	North Yorkshire Moors Railway	106
	Wensleydale Railway	109
Chapter 7	**North West**	111
	East Lancashire Railway	111
	Lakeside & Haverthwaite Railway	115
Chapter 8	**North East**	117
	Weardale Railway	117
Chapter 9	**Scotland**	119
	Bo'ness & Kinneil Railway	119
	Strathspey Railway	122
Chapter 10	**Wales**	124
	Llangollen Railway	124
	Pontypool and Blaenavon Railway	126
Appendix	**Other Preserved Railways**	128

Introduction

Welcome to what we hope will be a regularly updated and expanded guide to the world of preserved railways in the UK. Here, we have attempted to pull together all the information that enthusiasts find most useful when visiting heritage railways, including:

- A full stocklist of all locomotives and multiple units, with their current statuses and liveries.
- A brief history of the preserved railway itself.
- A map of the line, with miles and chains in order for mileages to be calculated by any travelling visitors.
- Gradient profiles, for visitors to identify sections where the locomotives may need to be worked hard and provide more entertaining sounds and possibly sights.
- Prospects for expansion of facilities and running lines.
- Refreshments, with a guide to local recommended pubs.

Much of this information has not been published before and placing all this together in one place makes for a handy field guide for enthusiasts, and even non-enthusiast visitors, to Britain's major preservation centres.

Space has not permitted all lines to be included in this issue or details, such as hauled coaching stock, wagons and other rolling stock. The stocklists were, as far as could be researched, up to date to the end of November 2021. It is recommended that you check the websites for the various railways before planning your visit.

Thanks go to the many railways that responded to requests for information, also Stuart Clarke, whose excellent publication *Great Britain Miles and Chains (Kilometre by Kilometre)* was the reference material for most of the quoted distances on the detailed maps. For anyone interested in his publication, and his other tables of mileages for Great Britain and the whole world, he can be contacted at stuart_clarke15@hotmail.com.

Chapter 1
South West

Avon Valley Railway

The Avon Valley Railway (AVR) forms part of the former Midland Railway (MR) Mangotsfield and Bath branch, part of a through route between Birmingham and the south coast that opened in 1869 and later joined to the Somerset and Dorset Railway. The line was closed under Beeching in 1966. Starting in 1977, the line has gradually expanded to its current limits. The main operating and maintenance base is Bitton and 3 miles of track have been re-laid on the route from Avon Riverside, through Bitton, to Oldland Common.

Getting there: The closest rail station to Bitton is Keynsham on the Bristol–Westbury line, which is served by Cardiff Central to Portsmouth Harbour trains. Keynsham to Bitton is 1½ miles and walkable. The 318 bus service from Keynsham operates hourly Monday-Saturday from the stop opposite the station to Willsbridge (for the AVR). There is also a 17 bus from Keynsham or a 42 from Bristol (every 30 minutes, alight at Cherry Gardens Road). The line can also be accessed by bike via the Bristol and Bath Railway Path (Route 4 of the National Cycle Network). The path goes on to follow the AVR trackbed.

Refreshments: A buffet is available at Bitton Station, no real ale on site, although there is an annual beer festival. Pubs in Bitton are around a 1 mile walk away.

Future plans: Any expansion of the line would need to be agreed with Sustrans, the owners of the Bristol and Bath Railway Path and all of the potential expansion trackbed. Extension northwards is now checked by a housing development, but expansion work is planned to extend the railway a further 3 miles southeast towards Kelston and a proposed Bath Riverside station.

Website: https://www.avonvalleyrailway.org

D2994 (Class 07 07010) stands at Avon Riverside on 15 June 2005 on a service from Bitton.

Number(s) (Operating Number Highlighted)	Type	Status	Livery
Ex-BR Diesel Locos			
07010	Class 07	Undergoing repair	BR Blue
08202	Class 08	Operational	BR Blue
08359	Class 08	Operational	BR Blue
D4118 (**08888**)	Class 08	Undergoing overhaul	BR Green
09015	Class 09	Undergoing overhaul	Primer
5518 (**31101**)	Class 31	Operational	BR Blue
31130	Class 31	Operational	Railfreight Original Grey
Ex-Industrial Diesel Locos			
446 *Kingswood*	Andrew Barclay Sons and Co 0-4-0	Awaiting repairs	Green
610	Sentinel 0-8-0DH	Undergoing restoration	Blue
WD 70031	Andrew Barclay 0-4-0DM	Operational	Black
MOD 429	Ruston and Hornsby LSSH 0-6-0DH	Operational	Red
Diesel Multiple Units			
52006	Class 107 DMBS	Operational	BR Green
52025	Class 107 DMCL	Operational	BR Green
Ex-Main Line Steam Locos			
44123	LMS Fowler 4F	Undergoing restoration	Primer
Ex-Industrial Steam Locos			
WD132	Hunslet 0-6-0ST	Operational	WD Green
4015	Fablok Polish TkH 49 0-6-0T	Operational	PKP Green
1798	Avonside 0-6-0ST	Undergoing restoration	Primer
7492	Sentinel 4wd	Operational	Dark Blue
7151	Robert Stephen Hawthorn 0-6-0T	Restoration	Black
5	Manning Wardle 0-6-0ST	Stored	Dark Blue

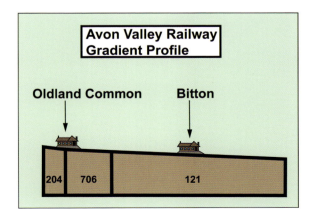

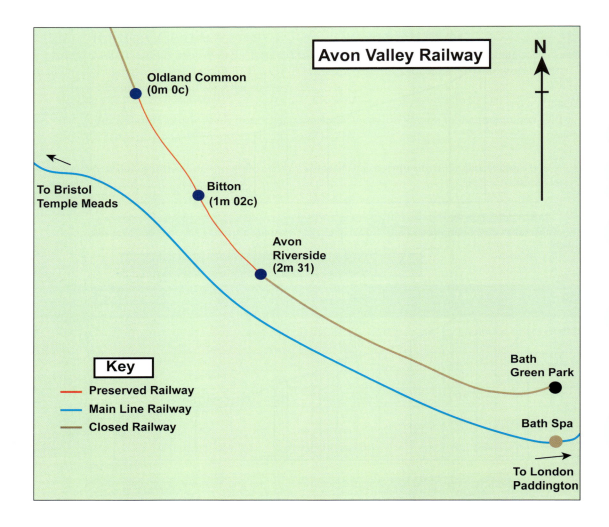

Bodmin & Wenford Railway

The railway, originally opened in 1887, operates two separate Great Western Railway (GWR) branch lines, totalling 6 miles in length, from Bodmin General to Bodmin Parkway (previously Bodmin Road) and to Boscarne, this extension opening in 1888. Passenger services were withdrawn in 1967, with closure to freight (to Wenfordbridge) from 1983. The line was reopened as far as Bodmin General in 1990 and on to Boscarne in 1997. The headquarters and main workshops are located at Bodmin General.

Getting there: Main line trains operate to and from Bodmin Parkway. By car, there is free parking at Bodmin General – PL31 1AG.

Refreshments: Cornish Rail Coffee Co, Bodmin General, pasties, sausage rolls; Signalbox Café, Bodmin Parkway, hot and cold food. Pub: Hole in The Wall, Bodmin town centre, 10 minutes' walk from General, former CAMRA Cornwall pub of the year, three changing beers.

Future plans: The line to Boscarne Junction lies on the former London and South Western Railway (LSWR) route to Wadebridge and Padstow, which is now the Camel Trail. The railway hopes to extend along this route towards Wadebridge in the future, although the current plan is a three-phase reopening, with initial extensions to Nanstallon Halt and Grogley Halt.

Website: https://bodminrailway.co.uk

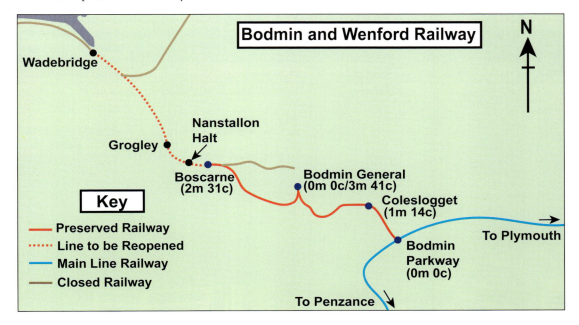

Number(s) (Operating Number Highlighted)	Type	Status	Livery
Ex-BR Diesel Locos			
08444	Class 08	Operational	BR Green
D3452	Class 10	Awaiting overhaul	BR Black
37142	Class 37	Undergoing overhaul	BR Blue
47306 *The Sapper*	Class 47	Operational	RfD European
50042 *Triumph*	Class 50	Operational	BR Large Logo Black Roof
Ex-Industrial Diesel Locos			
22928 *Peter*	Fowler 0-4-0DM	Operational	Green
443642 *Brian*	Ruston and Hornsby 0-4-0	Operational	Maroon
P403 *Denise*	Sentinel 0-6-0	Undergoing repairs	Orange
Diesel Multiple Units			
55020	Class 121 DMBS	Awaiting repairs	Chiltern Railways Blue
Ex-BR Steam Locos			
4247	GWR 4200 Class 2-8-0T	Awaiting overhaul	BR Unlined Black
4612	GWR 5700 Class 0-6-0PT	Operational	GWR Green
6435	GWR 600 Class 0-6-0PT	Awaiting overhaul	BR Lined Green
5552	GWR 4574 Class 2-6-2T	Restoration	Primer
Ex-Industrial Steam Locos			
2766	Hunslet Austerity 0-6-0ST	Operational	War Department Khaki
2572	Bagnall 0-4-0ST	Undergoing restoration	Port of Par Green
3058	Bagnall 0-4-0ST	Awaiting overhaul	Port of Par Green
19	Bagnall 0-4-0ST	Awaiting overhaul	HM Devonport Dockyard maroon

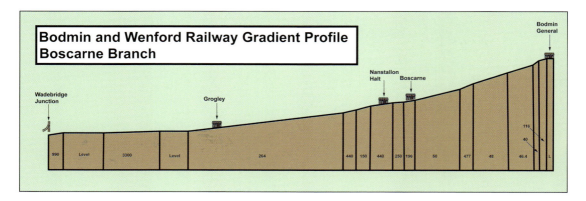

Bodmin and Wenford Railway Gradient Profile
Boscarne Branch

Dartmouth Steam Railway

Formerly the Paignton and Dartmouth Steam Railway, this line runs for 7 miles between Paignton and Kingswear (which has frequent ferries to Dartmouth) skirting the Torbay coast and the Dart Estuary. The main depot and workshops are at Churston. Originally opened as a broad-gauge line in 1859 and converted to standard gauge in 1892, it was closed by BR in 1972, reopening in the same year as an offshoot of the Dart Valley Railway.

Getting there: The main line station at Paignton adjoins the preserved railway terminus. Car parking – TQ4 6AF. The Totnes Steamer Quay also provides a unique way to get to Dartmouth.

Refreshments: Head of Steam Café, Paignton, drinks and snacks; Belle Bistro, Kingswear station. Pubs: Seven Stars, Dartmouth, 10 minutes' walk, guest beers and hot food; Henry's Bar, Paignton, guest beers, hot food.

Future plans: There is no room for track expansion with the full branch already being used.

Website: https://www.dartmouthrailriver.co.uk

Number(s) (Operating Number Highlighted)	Type	Status	Livery
Ex-BR Diesel Locos			
D2192 *Titan* (03192)	Class 03	Operational	BR Black
03371	Class 03	Operational	BR Blue
D3014 *Samson*	Class 08	Operational	BR Green
D6975 (37275)	Class 37	Operational	BR Blue
Diesel Multiple Units			
59719	Class 115 TCL	Stored	BR Green
59003	Class 116 TC	Operational as hauled stock	Chocolate/Cream
59004	Class 116 TC	Operational as hauled stock	Chocolate/Cream
59488	Class 117 TSL	Exhibition coach	Cream/Grey
59494	Class 117 TSL	Operational as hauled stock	Chocolate/Cream
59503	Class 117 TSL	Operational as hauled stock	Chocolate/Cream
59507	Class 117 TSL	Operational as hauled stock	Chocolate/Cream
59513	Class 117 TSL	Operational as hauled stock	Chocolate/Cream
59517	Class 117 TSL	Operational as hauled stock	Chocolate/Cream
Ex-BR Steam Locos			
4110	GWR 5101 Class 2-6-2T	Undergoing overhaul	GWR Green
4277 *Hercules*	GWR 4200 Class 2-8-0T	Undergoing overhaul	GWR Green
4555 *Warrior*	GWR 4500 Class 2-6-2T	Operational	GWR Green
5239 *Goliath*	GWR 5205 Class 2-8-0T	Operational	GWR Green
7827 *Lydham Manor*	GWR 7800 Class 4-6-0	Awaiting overhaul	BR Lined Black
75014 *Braveheart*	BR Standard 4 4-6-0	Operational	BR Lined Black
2253 *Omaha*	S160 2-8-0	Operational	Plum

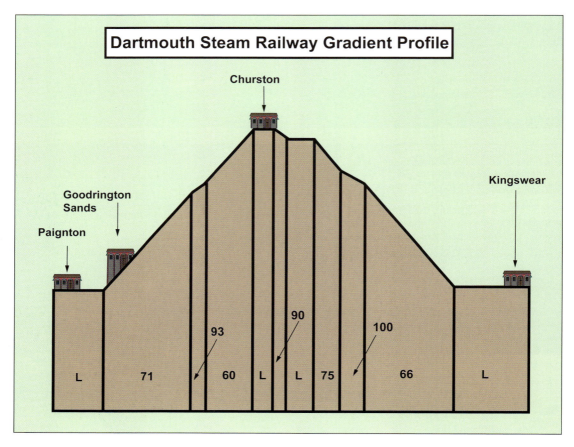

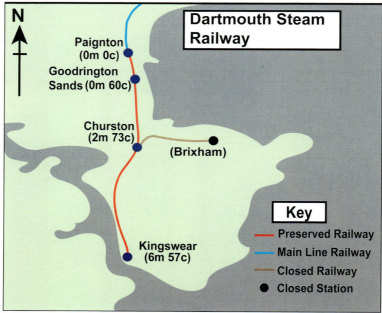

Restored to BR Blue, D402 (50002 *Superb***) passes Goodrington Sands in August 1995 on a train from Paignton to Dartmouth. (Andy Flowers Collection)**

Dean Forest Railway

Running 4¼ miles from Lydney to Parkend over the former horse-drawn tramway, the Dean Forest Railway was built by the Severn and Wye Railway in 1810. The main headquarters and workshops are located at Norchard. North of Parkend, the railway joined a complex network running to destinations including Cinderford, Lydbrook, Ross on Wye and on to Hereford.

Getting there: Lydney is served by main line services between Cardiff and Gloucester. Buses also operate from Gloucester to Lydney (number 23). Free car parking at Norchard – GL15 4ET.

Refreshments: Buffet at Norchard (snacks and drinks). Pub: The Miners Arms, Whitecroft, hot food and four guest beers.

Future plans: In 2016, the railway announced ambitious £8m plans to extend the line to Cinderford by 2023, adding over 10 miles of track length. The first step is likely to be Beechenhurst, an additional length of 2¾ miles from the current terminus at Parkend.

Website: https://deanforestrailway.co.uk

Well-travelled 20059 arrives at Parkend on 25 August 2017 with a train from Lydney Junction.

Number(s) (Operating Number Highlighted)	Type	Status	Livery
Ex-BR Diesel Locos			
08238 *Charlie*	Class 08	Operational	BR Blue
08473	Class 08	Spares donor, frame only	BR Blue
D3937 *Gladys* (08769)	Class 08	Operational	BR Green
D9521	Class 14	Operational	BR Blue
D9555	Class 14	Undergoing repair	BR Two-Tone Green
31210	Class 31	Undergoing overhaul	Primer
31235	Class 31	Stored	BR Blue
31466	Class 31	Operational	EWS Maroon/Gold
Ex-Industrial Diesel Locos			
4210127	Fowler 0-4-0DM	Stored	Grey
5622 *Don Corbett*	Hunslet 0-4-0	Operational	Departmental Yellow
6688 *Salty*	Hunslet 0-4-0	Undergoing overhaul	Red
3947 *Planet*	Hibberd 0-4-0DM	Undergoing overhaul	Green
Diesel Multiple Units			
50619	Class 108 DMBS	Undergoing maintenance	BR Green
51566	Class 108 DMCL	Undergoing maintenance	BR Green
51914	Class 108 DMBS	Operational	BR Green
52044	Class 108 DMCL	Spares donor	BR Blue/Grey
53632	Class 108 DMCL	Spares donor	BR Blue/Grey
56492	Class 108 DTCL	Operational	BR Green
59387	Class 108 TSL	Undergoing maintenance	BR Green
Ex-BR Steam Locos			
4575	GWR 4575 Class Small Prairie 2-6-2T	Operational	GWR Green
9681	GWR 8750 Class Pannier 0-6-0PT	Undergoing overhaul	BR Black
9682	GWR 8750 Class Pannier 0-6-0PT	Awaiting overhaul	BR Black
Ex-Industrial Steam Locos			
WD152 *Rennes*	RSH Austerity 0-6-0ST	Operational	Black
2147	Peckett R4 Class 0-4-0ST	Undergoing overhaul	Green
2413 *Gunby*	Hunslet 50550 Class 0-6-0ST	Undergoing overhaul	Primer
3806 *Wilbert*	Hunslet Austerity 0-6-0ST	Awaiting overhaul	Blue
3823 *Warrior*	Hunslet Austerity 0-6-0ST	Awaiting overhaul	Blue
2411 *Gloria*	Hunslet Austerity 0-6-0ST	Awaiting overhaul	Blue
65	Hunslet Austerity 0-6-0ST	Awaiting overhaul	Primer
2221	Andrew Barclay 0-4-0ST	Awaiting overhaul	Maroon

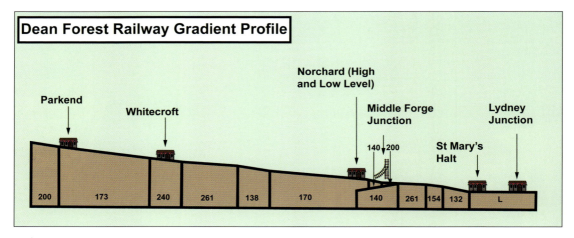

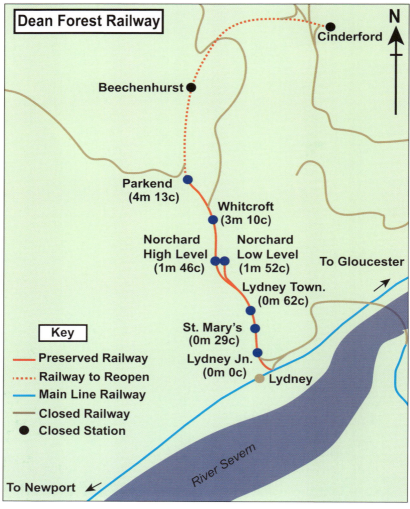

East Somerset Railway

The 2½-mile-long line runs from Cranmore to Mendip Vale and was built originally by the East Somerset Railway Company in 1858 as a 7ft ¼in broad-gauge line. Absorbed by the GWR in 1874, it was converted to standard gauge during the same year. The line, part of the Cheddar Valley Line from Witham to Yatton, was closed to passengers by BR in 1963 and freight in 1985, before reopening as a preserved line for passenger use in 1975. The railway is connected to the main line at Cranmore as part of the connection to Merehead Quarry (from Frome). The main workshops and headquarters are found at Cranmore.

Getting there: The nearest main line rail stations are Castle Cary and Frome. Cranmore village has a Monday–Friday bus service, number 161 from Frome to Shepton Mallet. Free parking at Cranmore – BA4 4QP.

Refreshments: The Whistlestop Café, Cranmore, full meals including breakfast. No pubs near the railway.

Future plans: The line may be extended over the next few years from Mendip Vale to Cannards Grave/Shepton Mallet East.

Website: https://eastsomersetrailway.com

Number(s) (Operating Number Highlighted)	Type	Status	Livery
Ex-Industrial Diesel Loco			
10165 *Joan*	Sentinel 0-4-0	Operational	Maroon
10175 DH16	Sentinel 0-4-0	Operational	Blue
10199 *Cattewater*	Sentinel 0-6-0	Operational	Red
10218 PBA 39	Sentinel 0-6-0	Operational	Blue
10221 PBA 42 *Eric*	Sentinel 0-6-0	Awaiting restoration	Blue
Diesel Multiple Units			
51909	Class 108 DMBS	Operational	BR Blue
51947	Class 108 DMBS	Spares donor	Green
54271	Class 108 DTCL	Operational	BR Blue
Electric Multiple Units			
129	Class 483 DMSO	Awaiting restoration	London Transport Maroon
Ex-BR Steam Locos			
46447	Ivatt Class 2 2-6-0	Operational	BR Black
4555	GWR 4500 Class 2-6-2T Small Prairie	Operational	GWR Green
4110	GWR 5101 Class 2-6-2T	Undergoing restoration	GWR Green
Ex-Industrial Steam Loco			
1719 *Lady Nan*	Barclay 0-4-0ST	Operational	Blue
31 *Meteor*	RSH 0-6-0T	Awaiting restoration	Red

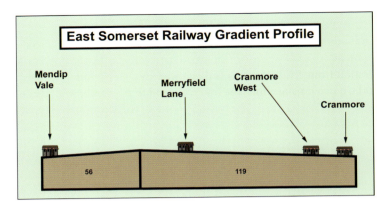

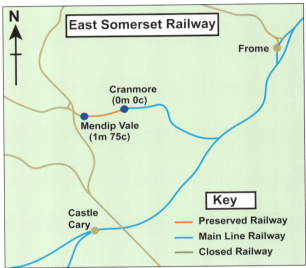

BR Standard Class 9F 92203 *Black Prince* is prepared for duty at Cranmore on 15 August 1983. Overhaul, maintenance and operation of steam locomotives is labour intensive and requires many hours of work from volunteers on preserved lines. (Andy Flowers Collection)

Gloucestershire Warwickshire Steam Railway

The preserved line operates over part of the former GWR main line from Birmingham to Cheltenham via Stratford-Upon-Avon, which was opened in 1906 and closed in 1976 by BR. The line reopened as a preserved operation from Toddington to Hayes Abbey in 1984. The main base is at Toddington, with workshops and a narrow-gauge line. The line reopened to Cheltenham Racecourse in 2003 and Broadway in 2018.

Getting there: Stagecoach services D and E run every ten minutes Monday–Saturday and every 30 minutes on Sundays from Cheltenham Spa main line station to Cheltenham Racecourse (5 to 10 minutes' walk from the GWR station). Routes 606, 606S, W1 and W2 run from Cheltenham Royal Well bus station to Winchcombe and Toddington. Free car parking at Cheltenham Racecourse – GL50 4SH – and Toddington – GL54 5DT.

Refreshments: Toddington station, full buffet serving hot meals. Pub: The Pheasant Inn, Toddington, 2 minutes' walk, Donnington beers, hot food.

Future plans: Longer-term plans include reopening towards Cheltenham (with a main line connection) and extending the line north from Broadway towards Stratford-Upon-Avon, starting with the 6 mile section to Honeybourne.

Website: https://www.gwsr.com

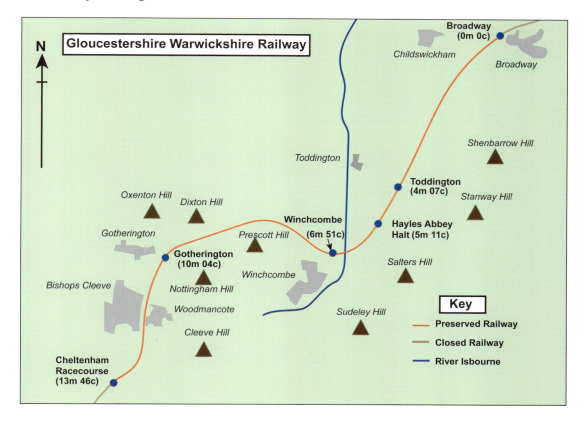

Number(s) (Operating Number Highlighted)	Type	Status	Livery
Ex-BR Diesel Locos			
D2182	Class 03	Operational	BR Green
D2280	Class 04	Undergoing restoration	Primer
D8137 (20137)	Class 20	Operational	BR Green
20228	Class 20	Undergoing restoration	BR Blue
20035	Class 20	Stored	Orange and White CFD
24081	Class 24	Operational	BR Blue
D5343 (26043)	Class 26	Undergoing overhaul	BR Blue
37215	Class 37	Operational	BR Blue
D6948 (37248)	Class 37	Undergoing overhaul	BR Green
45149	Class 45	Operational	BR Blue
47105	Class 47	Operational	BR Blue
47376 *Freightliner 1995*	Class 47	Operational	BR Freightliner Grey
Ex-Industrial Diesel Locos			
11230	Drewry 0-6-0DM	Operational	BR Black
372 *Des* (YE2760)	Yorkshire 0-6-0DE	Operational	Blue with Wasp Stripes
Diesel Multiple Units			
52029	Class 107 DMCL	Stored	Strathclyde Black and Orange
51363	Class 117 DMBS	Operational	BR Green
59510	Class 117 TCL	Operational	BR Green
51405	Class 117 DMS	Operational	BR Green
51360	Class 117 DMBS	Undergoing restoration	BR Blue
51372	Class 117 DMBS	Awaiting restoration	BR Blue
59505	Class 117 TCL	Awaiting restoration	BR Green
55003	Class 122 DMBS	Undergoing restoration	BR Green
Ex-BR Steam Locos			
2807	GWR 2800 Class 2-8-0	Undergoing overhaul	GWR Green
2874	GWR 2800 Class 2-8-0	Undergoing restoration	Primer
3850	GWR 2884 Class 2-8-0	Undergoing overhaul	BR Unlined Black
4270	GWR 4200 Class 2-8-0T	Operational	GWR Green
7820 *Dinmore Manor*	GWR 7800 Manor Class 4-6-0	Operational	BR Lined Black
7903 *Foremarke Hall*	GWR 6959 Class Modified Hall 4-6-0	Operational	BR Green
35006 *Peninsular and Oriental S. N. Co.*	SR Merchant Navy Class 4-6-2	Operational	BR Green
76077	BR Standard 4MT 2-6-0	Undergoing restoration	BR Black
Ex-Industrial Steam Locos			
1976 *John*	Peckett 0-4-0ST	Static	Blue

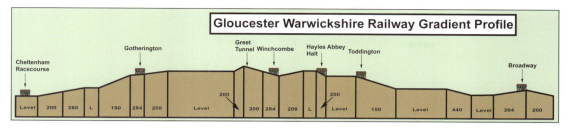

Right: Southern Railway Merchant Navy 35006 *Peninsular and Oriental S. N. Co.* approaches Cheltenham Racecourse with a train from Toddington on the Gloucestershire and Warwickshire Railway on 5 June 2021.

Below: 7903 *Foremarke Hall* waits at Cheltenham Racecourse with a train for Toddington on 30 December 2018, during the Gloucestershire and Warwickshire Railway's Christmas gala.

South Devon Railway

Originally opened by the GWR as a broad-gauge line in 1872 and converted to standard gauge in 1892, the South Devon Railway (SDR) was reopened in 1969 and runs for 6¾ miles from Totnes to Buckfastleigh, mostly along the River Dart. It was known as the Dart Valley Railway until 1991.

Getting there: The Totnes heritage railway station is a short walk from the main line one. Buses from Exeter and Plymouth also serve Buckfastleigh (X64). Free car parking at Buckfastleigh – TQ11 0DZ.

Refreshments: Hot meals in the buffet at Buckfastleigh. Pubs: The Dartbridge Inn, Buckfastleigh, 5 minutes' walk, guest beer, hot food; The Totnes Brewing Co, Totnes, guest beers, no hot food.

Future plans: There are long-term plans to extend the railway to Ashburton, the original terminus of the branch, and these have been boosted by the dropping of plans for redevelopment of the station area there.

Website: https://www.southdevonrailway.co.uk

DMUs provide many services on heritage railways, particularly out of season. On 24 August 2013, Class 122, driving motor brake second (DMBS) 55000, runs empty into Buckfastleigh.

Number(s) (Operating Number Highlighted)	Type	Status	Livery
Ex-BR Diesel Locos			
D2246	Class 04	Operational	BR Green
D2271	Class 04	Operational	BR Green
D3721 (09010)	Class 09	Operational	BR Black
D7535 (25185)	Class 25	Awaiting repair	BR Blue
D7541 (25191)	Class 25	Awaiting repair	BR Two-Tone Green
D7612 (25262)	Class 25	Operational	BR Two-Tone Green
33002 *Sea King*	Class 33	Operational	Departmental Grey
6737 (37037)	Class 37	Awaiting overhaul	BR Blue
50002	Class 50	Undergoing overhaul	Primer
Ex-Industrial Diesel Locos			
LO52 (2745)	Yorkshire 0-6-0DE	Awaiting repair	Green
MFP 4	John Fowler and Co. 0-4-0DM	Awaiting repair	Red
418793 *Dusty*	Ruston and Hornsby 0-4-0DH	Operational	Green
Diesel Multiple Units			
59740	Class 115 TS	Static bar coach	Maroon
51352	Class 117 DMBS	Awaiting restoration	Yellow
59493	Class 117 TCL	Awaiting restoration	BR Green
51376	Class 117 DMS	Awaiting restoration	BR Green
55000	Class 122 DMBS	Operational	BR Green
Ex-BR Steam Locos			
1420	GWR 1400 Class 0-4-2T	Undergoing overhaul	GWR Green
136	GWR 1366 Class 0-6-0PT	Operational	GWR Green
3205	GWR 2251 Class 0-6-0	Awaiting overhaul	GWR Green
3803	GWR 2884 Class 2-8-0	Awaiting overhaul	GWR Green
5526	GWR 4575 Class 2-6-2T	Operational	GWR Green
5542	GWR 4575 Class 2-6-2T	Operational	GWR Green
5786	GWR 5700 Class 0-6-0PT	Operational	LT Maroon
6412	GWR 6400 Class 0-6-0PT	Operational	BR Lined Green
Ex-Industrial Steam Locos			
1 *Ashley*	Peckett 0-4-0ST	Static	Green
Lee Moor No 2	Peckett 0-4-0ST	Static	Green
1690 *Lady Angela*	Peckett 0-4-0ST	Awaiting overhaul	Green
47 *Carnarvon*	Kitson and Co. 0-6-0ST	Undergoing overhaul	Blue
3810 *Glendower*	Hunslet 0-6-0ST	Awaiting overhaul	Blue

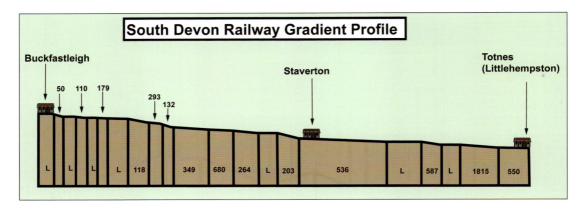

20110 waits at Totnes on 24 August 2013 with a train for Buckfastleigh, South Devon Railway.

Swanage Railway

The Swanage Railway runs from Wareham to Swanage and is operated as a preserved line from Norden. The line, branching from the main Weymouth to London route at Worgret Junction, 1 mile west of Wareham, was opened by the Swanage Railway in 1885, being absorbed into the LSWR the following year. BR withdrew passenger services in 1972, with freight carrying on to Furzebrook Sidings. The line reopened as a heritage railway in 1979 with a short stretch from Swanage, which was extended to Harmans Cross in 1988 and through to Norden in 1995. The preserved line was reconnected to the national network on 3 January 2002, with track joined at Motala (near Furzebrook) exactly 30 years after the closure of the Swanage branch. The main workshops and depot are at Swanage.

Getting there: Wareham is the nearest rail station with half-hourly services from Weymouth and Waterloo. Bus service 40 from Wareham is hourly to Corfe and Swanage Monday–Saturday and summer Sundays, and two-hourly at other times. Bus number 50 runs from Bournemouth to Swanage via the Sandbanks Ferry every hour Monday–Saturday in summer with open top buses. Parking at Norden (pay and display) – BH20 5DW.

Refreshments: Full hot food buffet at Swanage. Pub: Red Lion, Swanage, ten minutes' walk, full food menu and guest beers. A beer festival is held at Norden in conjunction with the May diesel gala.

Future Plans: In 2006, the Swanage Railway signed a connection agreement with the national railway network. Since 2009, the Network Rail line from Worgret Junction to Motala has been used by excursion traffic. Worgret Junction was upgraded in 2012 with a new track layout, enabling passenger trains from Swanage and Corfe Castle to run on to Wareham. In 2013, the railway gained a £1.4m government grant to return passenger trains between Swanage and Wareham. Negotiations are taking place with Network Rail and Dorset County Council for this connecting service using Class 117 Diesel Multiple Units to start.

Website: https://www.swanagerailway.co.uk

On 8 May 2009, during the Swanage Railway's highly popular annual diesel gala and beer festival, 55022 *Royal Scots Grey* passes Corfe Castle with a service from Swanage to Norden.

Number(s) (Operating Number Highlighted)	Type	Status	Livery
Ex-BR Diesel Locos			
D3551 (**08436**)	Class 08	Operational	LSWR Black
D3591 (**08476**)	Class 08	Operational	BR Green
D6515 (**33012**)	Class 33	Undergoing repairs (at Eastleigh Works)	BR Green
33111	Class 33	Operational	BR Blue
Ex-Industrial Diesel Locos			
4210132	Fowler 0-4-0DM	Undergoing restoration	Non-standard white
Beryl	FC Hibberd Planet	To be Plinthed	Non-standard green
Diesel Multiple Units			
51356	Class 117 DMBS	Operational	BR Green
59486	Class 117 TCL	Operational	BR Green
51388	Class 117 DMS	Operational	BR Green
51392	Class 117 DMS	Spares donor	Network SouthEast
55028	Class 121 DMBS	Operational	BR Green
Electric Multiple Units			
69332	Class 422 4-BIG TSRB	Awaiting restoration	BR Green
76298	Class 438 4-TC DTSO	Stored	London Transport Maroon
70855	Class 438 4-TC TFK	Awaiting restoration	London Transport Maroon
70824	Class 438 4-TC TBSK	Undergoing restoration	BR Blue/Grey
76275	Class 438 4-TC DTSO	Restored	BR Blue/Grey
76322	Class 438 4-TC DTSO	Undergoing restoration	BR Blue/Grey
Ex-BR Steam Locos			
563	LSWR Adams T3 4-4-0	Undergoing overhaul	LSWR Green
30120	LSWR T9 Class 4-4-0	Stored	BR Lined Black
30053	LSWR Class M7 0-4-4T	Undergoing overhaul	BR Lined Black
31625	SR U Class 2-6-0	Stored	BR Lined Black
31874	SR N Class 2-6-0	Undergoing overhaul	Primer
31806	SR U Class 2-6-0	Operational	BR Lined Black
34010 *Sidmouth*	SR West Country Class 4-6-2	Undergoing restoration	
34070 *Manston*	SR Battle of Britain Class 4-6-2	Operational	BR Lined Green
34072 *257 Squadron*	SR Battle of Britain Class 4-6-2	Operational	BR Lined Green
34028 *Eddystone*	SR West Country Class 4-6-2	Operational	BR Lined Green
35025 *Brocklebank Line*	SR Merchant Navy Class 4-6-2	Stored	
80104	BR Standard 4MT 2-6-4T	Undergoing overhaul	BR Lined Black
Ex-Industrial Steam Locos			
69 *Norman*	Hunslet Austerity 0-6-0ST	Undergoing overhaul	Black

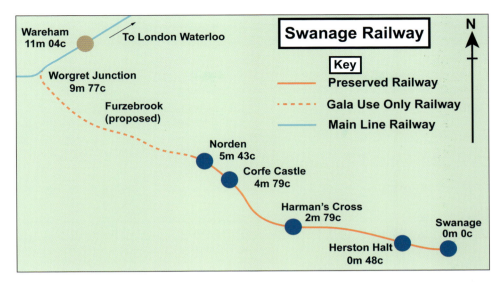

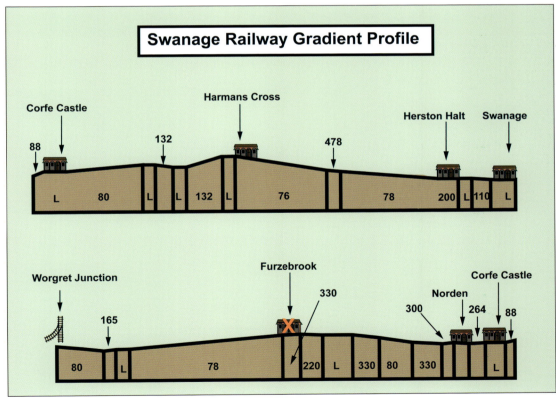

Swindon & Cricklade Railway

Opened between 1884 and 1891, as part of the Midland and South Western Junction Railway from Cheltenham to Andover via Swindon, the line closed to passengers in 1961 and to goods between 1964 and 1970. The preserved operation began in 1985, with extensions from Blunsdon to South Meadow in 2008 and Taw Valley Halt in 2014. Headquarters for the 2½-mile line is at Blunsdon.

Getting there: Thamesdown Transport runs bus services from Swindon to Queen Elizabeth Drive and the railway's Taw Valley Halt. Numbers are 15 and 15A Monday–Saturday, with Stagecoach service 19 on Sundays and Bank Holidays. Free car parking at Blunsdon – SN25 2DA.

Refreshments: A Norwegian café coach together with a buffet is based at Blunsdon. No nearby pubs.

Future plans: A northern extension is planned, initially to Farfield Lane, then later to Cricklade. Southwards, the line is to be extended to Mouldon Hill, then further towards Swindon.

Website: swindon-cricklade-railway.org

Number(s) (Operating Number Highlighted)	Type	Status	Livery
Ex-BR Diesel Locos			
03022	Class 03	Operational	Non-Standard Blue
D2152 (03152)	Class 03	Operational	BR Green
D3261	Class 08	Operational	BR Green
D3668 (09004)	Class 09	Operational	BR Blue
E6003 *Sir Herbert Walker* (73003)	Class 73	Operational	BR Green
PWM651 (97651)	Class 97/6	Operational	BR Green
Ex-Industrial Diesel Locos			
4220031	Fowler 0-4-0DH	Operational	Blue
7342	Fowler 0-4-0DM	Operational	Orange
21442	Fowler 0-4-0DM	Operational	Blue
Diesel Multiple Units			
59514	Class 117 TCL	Stored	BR Green
51074	Class 119 DMBC	Operational	BR Green
51104	Class 119 DMSL	Operational	BR Green
79978	AC Cars Railbus	Awaiting overhaul	BR Green
Diesel Electric Multiple Units			
60669	Class 205 TS	Awaiting restoration	Network SouthEast
60822	Class 205 DTCL	Undergoing restoration	Primer
60127	Class 207 DMBSO	Awaiting restoration	BR Green
Ex-Industrial Steam Locos			
2138	Andrew Barclay 0-6-0ST	Operational	Black
3135	Fablok TKh49 0-6-0T	Repairs	Red
70	Hudswell Clarke 0-6-0T	Overhaul	Slate Grey
2354	Andrew Barclay 0-4-0ST	Overhaul	Blue

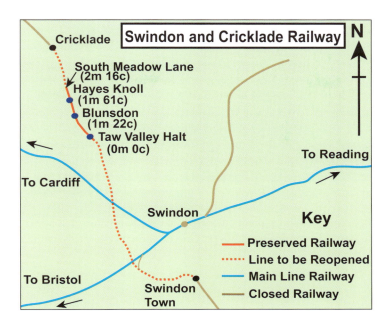

W6-S Class Peckett 0-4-0ST No 1967 *Merlin* stands at Blunsdon during its stay at the Swindon & Cricklade Railway on 15 August 1993. Preserved railways in the UK are home to a large number of ex-industrial preserved tank engines, in addition to larger ex-main line types.

West Somerset Railway

The route was originally opened as a broad-gauge line in 1862 between Taunton and Watchet by the Bristol and Exeter Railway. In 1874, it was extended from Watchet to Minehead by the Minehead Railway and was converted to standard gauge in 1882, before absorption by the GWR in 1890. Despite buoyant summer traffic, the line was unprofitable and was closed by BR in 1971, reopening as a heritage line in 1976 between Minehead and Blue Anchor. By 1979, the whole line to Bishops Lydeard was in use. At 20½ miles between Minehead and Bishops Lydeard, the West Somerset Railway (WSR) is advertised as the longest heritage railway in England and the longest standard gauge preserved line in the UK. Somerset County Council owns the track and stations, which are leased to the WSR. At gala events, some services operate over the 2½ miles from Bishops Lydeard to Norton Fitzwarren, the connection to the main line that enables through trains to operate onto Network Rail. Most diesel locomotives are housed and maintained at the DEPG depot at Williton, with some industrial shunters out-stationed at locations along the line. Steam is maintained at Williton and Minehead.

Getting there: First Somerset and Avon service number 28 runs from the South Side Interchange at Taunton station to Bishops Lydeard on operating days. Future events may include DMU shuttles running between Taunton and Bishops Lydeard. Free car park at Bishops Lydeard.

Refreshments: Turntable café at Minehead station, hot food and drinks. Pub: Quantock Brewery, opposite Bishops Lydeard station, Quantock beers, food on Fridays and Saturdays only.

Future Plans: The branch nature of the route restricts extensions but longer-term plans to operate into Taunton are regularly considered.

Website: www.west-somerset-railway.co.uk

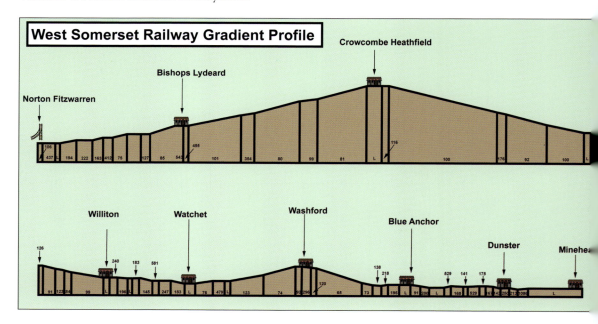

Number(s) (Operating Number Highlighted)	Type	Status	Livery
Ex-BR Diesel Locos			
D2133	Class 03	Operational	BR Green
D4107 (09019)	Class 09	Operational	BR Green
9518	Class 14	Long-term restoration	NCB Blue
D9526	Class 14	Operational	BR Two-Tone Green
D6566 (33048)	Class 33	Operational	BR Green
D6575 (33057)	Class 33	Operational	BR Green
D7017	Class 35	Operational	BR Green
D7018	Class 35	Operational	BR Green
47077 *North Star* (47840)	Class 47	Operational	BR Blue
D1010 *Western Campaigner*	Class 52	Undergoing repair	BR Maroon
Ex-Industrial Diesel Locos			
DH16	Sentinel 0-4-0	Operational	MSC Blue
578	Andrew Barclay 0-4-0DH	Operational	Non-standard Green
579	Andrew Barclay 0-4-0DH	Operational	Non-standard Green
24	Ruston and Hornsby 0-4-0DM	Operational	Green with Red Frames
200793 *Gower Princess*	Ruston and Hornsby 0-4-0DM	Operational	Brunswick Green
Diesel Multiple Units			
51859	Class 115 DMBS	Operational	BR Green
59678	Class 115 TCL	Operational	BR Green
51880	Class 115 DMBS	Operational	BR Green
51887	Class 115 DMBS	Stored	Non-standard Carmine and Cream
51354	Class 117 DMBS	Stored	BR Green
Ex-BR Steam Locos			
4561	GWR 4500 Class Small Prairie 2-6-2T	Undergoing overhaul	BR Black
5199	GWR 5101 Class Large Prairie 2-6-2T	Operational	GWR Green
7821 *Ditcheat Manor*	GWR 7800 Class Manor 4-6-0	Static display at Swindon	BR Lined Black
7822 *Foxcote Manor*	GWR 7800 Class Manor 4-6-0	Operational	GWR Green
7828 *Odney Manor*	GWR 7800 Class Manor 4-6-0	Operational	BR Lined Green
4936 *Kinlet Hall*	GWR 4900 Class Hall	Undergoing overhaul	TBC
9351	GWR 9351 Mogul 2-6-0	Operational	BR Lined Green
6024 *King Edward I*	GWR 6000 Class King 4-6-0	Awaiting repair	BR Lined Green
Ex-Industrial Steam Locos			
1788 *Kilmersdon*	Peckett R3 Class 0-4-0ST	Undergoing overhaul	S&DJR Blue

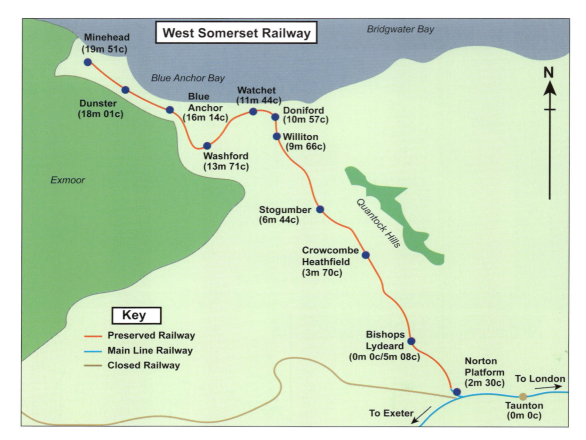

Above left: Visiting Class 25 D7535, otherwise known as 25185 from the Dartmouth Steam Railway, stands at Williton on 21 June 2019.

Above right: At the West Somerset Railway gala on 11 June 2017, guest locos D8188 and D8059 leave Blue Anchor on a Bishops Lydeard to Minehead service.

Chapter 2

South East

Bluebell Railway

This 11-mile line operates from East Grinstead to Sheffield Park and was the first standard gauge UK passenger line taken over by enthusiasts, being reopened in 1960. Originally opened in 1882 as part of the London, Brighton and South Coast Railway, the line included a branch from Horsted Keynes to Haywards Heath, which closed in 1963. North of Horsted Keynes, the 780-yard Sharpthorne Tunnel is the longest in preservation. The line was reopened to East Grinstead in 2013. Historically very anti-modern traction, the last few years have seen the start of annual diesel galas.

Getting there: Main line trains operate to East Grinstead from London Victoria. If driving, Sheffield Park is the best option with free parking and a large car park – TN22 3QL. Substantial car parking is also available in a field at Horsted Keynes station – RH17 7BB.

Refreshments: Pubs: Bessemer Arms at Sheffield Park station, hot food and guest beers; The Engine Room – Brewery Tap & Bar, East Grinstead, 15 minutes' walk, no hot food.

Future plans: The Bluebell purchased the trackbed from Horsted Keynes to the Railtrack boundary at Ardingley in 1997 with extension to here, or to the main line at Haywards Heath, a long-term aim. The line from Haywards Heath currently serves an active aggregates terminal, although trains could run adjacent to this. There have been suggestions of electrifying the branch, if reopened, for the use of preserved Electric Multiple Units (EMUs) and DC electric locos. South of Sheffield Park, any extension would need a bridge over the A275 and a cutting infilled with domestic waste. This would be a very long-term project, although the railway has aspirations for extending to Lewes via Newick and Chailey and Barcombe.

Website: www.bluebell-railway.com

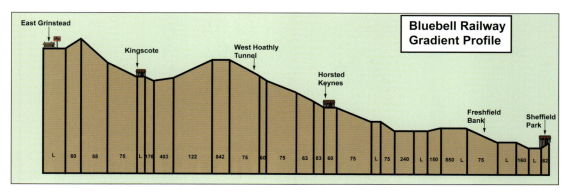

Number(s) (Operating Number Highlighted)	Type	Status	Livery
Ex-BR Diesel Locos			
D4106 (**09018**)	Class 09	Operational	BR Green
D6570 (**33052**)	Class 33	Awaiting restoration	BR Green
Ex-Industrial Diesel Locos			
10241	Sentinel 0-6-0	Operational	Green
957	4w Howard Class 2	Operational	Green
Ex-BR Steam Locos			
65	SER Stirling O1 Class 0-6-0	Operational	SECR Green
672 *Fenchurch*	LBSCR Class A1 'Terrier' 0-6-0T	Undergoing overhaul	Brown
263	SECR Class H 0-4-4T	Operational	SECR Green
A27	SECR P Class 0-6-0T	Undergoing overhaul	SECR Green
928 *Stowe*	SR V Class Schools 4-6-0	Undergoing overhaul	SR Green
30541	SR Maunsell Q Class 0-6-0	Operational	BR Black
847	SR Maunsell S15 Class 4-6-0	Operational	Southern Green
34059 *Sir Archibald Sinclair*	SR Rebuilt Battle of Britain Class 4-6-2	Undergoing overhaul	BR Green
80151	BR Standard 4MT 2-6-4T	Operational	BR Lined Black
73082 *Camelot*	BR Standard 5MT	Operational	BR Lined Black
New Build Locos			
32424 *Beachy Head*	LBSCR Class H2 4-4-2	Undergoing construction	To be decided
84030 (was 78059 in BR service)	BR Standard Class 2 2-6-2T	Conversion underway	Primer

On the evening of 15 April 2015, South Eastern and Chatham Railway H Class 0-4-4T 263 stands at Sheffield Park with the evening Pullman dining train, showing the atmospheric effects of steam and the original station gas lighting.

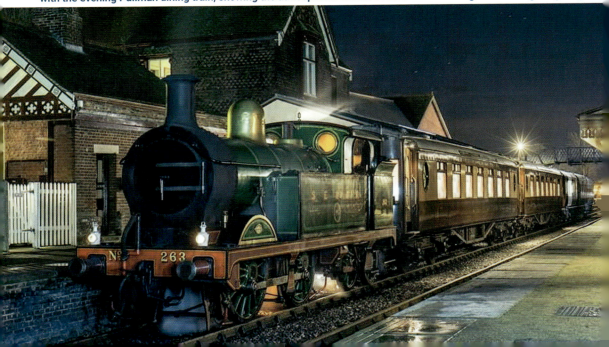

South East

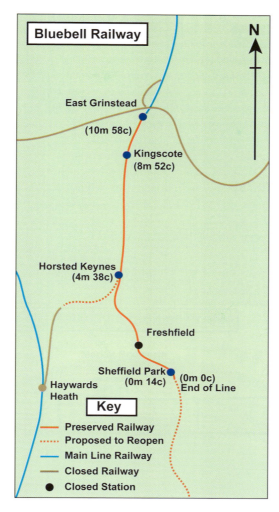

Historically, the Bluebell Railway had always been very much a steam-only operation, although the assistance of a number of diesels in the building of the extension to East Grinstead softened views somewhat and today the line even sees occasional diesel galas. In one of the first of such events, 20205 and 20189 arrive at Sheffield Park on 1 April 2017.

Chinnor & Princes Risborough Railway

Originally built as a light railway by the Watlington and Princes Risborough Railway Company from the GWR line at Princes Risborough for 8¾ miles to Watlington, the line from Princes Risborough continued on to Oxford, diverging at Thame Junction. Opened in 1872, the line was absorbed by the GWR in 1883. The line closed to passengers in 1957, closing for freight from Chinnor to Watlington in 1961. The line to Chinnor was retained for the cement works up until 1989. The line reopened from Chinnor in 1994, extending to Thame Junction in 1996 and finally through to Princes Risborough in 2018.

Getting there: An interchange platform exists between the Chiltern Main Line and the heritage railway at Princes Risborough. Chinnor, free parking – OX39 4ER.

Refreshments: Café (in rolling stock) at Chinnor, hot snacks and drinks. Pubs: The Crown, Station Road, Chinnor, five minutes' walk, food and Fuller's beers; Bird in Hand, Princes Risborough, 10 minutes' walk, guest beers but no food.

Future plans: The connection has now been made to the former Thame branch, which is still in use by Network Rail and Chiltern Railways as a siding. The railway is to purchase a lease of Network Rail land at Princes Risborough and the remaining section of the former Chinnor branch, then to replace the platform and track along the parallel formation. Chiltern Railways are also expanding and may eventually run trains to Milton Keynes and Bedford with more opportunities for interchange with the preserved line. Following this, the railway may extend to Aston Rowant.

Website: www.chinnorrailway.co.uk

Number(s) (Operating Number Highlighted)	Type	Status	Livery
Ex-BR Diesel Locos			
D3018 *Haversham* (**08011**)	Class 08	Operational	BR Green
08825	Class 08	Operational	Network SouthEast
D8568	Class 17	Operational	BR Blue
97205 (**31163**)	Class 31	Undergoing repair	BR Research
37227	Class 37	Operational	Railfreight Metals
Ex-Industrial Diesel Locos			
AD40 (WD8214/459515)	Ruston LSSH WD Class C3SA 0-6-0DH	Operational	Blue
Diesel Multiple Units			
977992 (**51375**)	Class 117 DMS (converted to watercannon centre car)	Source of spares and storage	Chiltern Green
55023	Class 121 DMBS	Undergoing repair	BR Green
55024	Class 121 DMBS	Operational	BR Maroon
Electric Multiple Units			
1198 (61736 + 70573 + 61737)	Class 411 3-CEP DMSO + TBCK + DMSO	Used as hauled stock	BR Blue

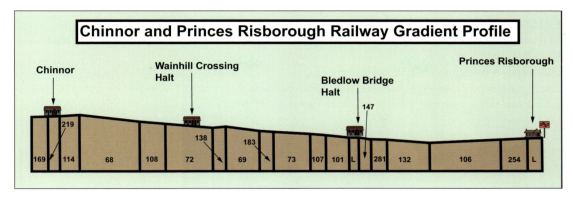

Class 17 Clayton D8568 rescues visiting D7535 approaching Chinnor on 5 April 2019 during the line's diesel gala. The Class 25 failed at the precise moment the author had pressed the shutter!

Cholsey & Wallingford Railway

Running between Cholsey and Wallingford, this former GWR branch line runs through 2½ miles of pleasant countryside, using a variety of Class 08s and ex-industrial steam locos. The branch was opened in 1866 by the Wallingford and Whatlington Railway, sold to the GWR in 1872, and closed for passengers by BR in 1959, although it was retained for freight traffic to Wallingford Maltings up to 1981. Upon closure, preservation efforts began with the first trains operated in 1985 and the full branch reopened in 1997.

Getting there: GWR serves Cholsey on the line between Didcot and Reading. Buses also run from Reading and Oxford. Car parking at Wallingford – OX10 9GQ.

Refreshments: Coffee shop at the front of Wallingford station. Pub: Royal Standard, Wallingford, local beers and food.

Future plans: Although the last segment of the line has been built over at the Wallingford end of the branch, a permanent station is planned at the current terminus.

Website: www.cholsey-wallingford-railway.com

Number(s) (Operating Number Highlighted)	Type	Status	Livery
Ex-BR Diesel Locos			
08022 *Lion*	Class 08	Operational	Guinness Black
08060 *Unicorn*	Class 08	Operational	Guinness Black
D3190 *George Mason* (08123)	Class 08	Operational	BR Green
Ex-Industrial Diesel Locos			
3270 *Carpenter*	Hibberd 0-4-0DM	Undergoing restoration	Black

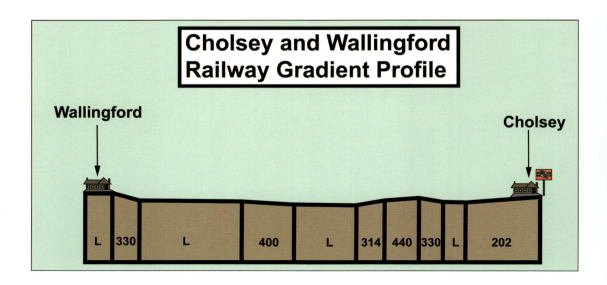

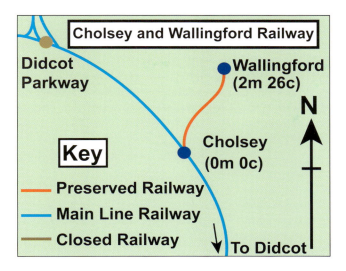

Class 08 diesel shunters have long been the staple home-based motive power on the Cholsey and Wallingford Railway. 08123 *George Mason* approaches Wallingford with a train from Cholsey on 24 June 2007.

Didcot Railway Centre

The Great Western Society took over the former Didcot locomotive depot in 1967, and in the 1970s it negotiated a long-term lease with BR. The GWR Museum based at Didcot has several short demonstration running lines around the site.

Getting there: A short footpath leads from Didcot Parkway main line station to the museum via a subway. Free car parking on surrounding streets – OX11 7NJ.

Refreshments: Buffet within site (hot food). Pub: Prince of Wales, opposite main line station, two changing beers, hot food.

Future plans: A new 50-year lease was signed with Network Rail in 2011. There is no option for running line expansion other than within the site, with more siding space being recently leased from DB Schenker.

Website: www.didcotrailwaycentre.org.uk

Number(s) (Operating Number Highlighted)	Type	Status	Livery
Ex-BR Diesel Locos			
08604 *Phantom*	Class 08	Operational	BR Blue
D9516	Class 14	Operational	BR Two-Tone Green
Gas Turbine Loco			
18000	Brown Boveri Gas Turbine	Static exhibit	BR Green
Ex-Industrial Diesel Locos			
DL26	Hunslet 0-6-0DM	Operational	BR Green
Ex-GWR Diesel Railcar			
22	GWR Diesel Railcar	Operational	GWR Chocolate/Cream
Ex-BR Steam Locos			
1338	Cardiff Railway/GWR Kitsons 0-4-0ST	Static	GWR Green
1340 *Trojan*	Avonside 0-4-0ST	Operational	GWR Green
1363	GWR 1361 Class 0-6-0ST	Awaiting restoration	GWR Green
1466 (4866)	GWR 1400 Class 0-4-2T	Undergoing overhaul	GWR Green
4144	GWR 4100 Class 2-6-2T	Operational	GWR Green
3650	GWR 5700 Class 0-6-0PT	Undergoing overhaul	GWR Green
3738	GWR 5700 Class 0-6-0PT	Static	GWR Green
3822	GWR 2884 Class 2-8-0	Static	GWR Black
4079 *Pendennis Castle*	GWR 4073 Class Castle 4-6-0	Undergoing restoration	GWR Green
5051 *Drysllwyn Castle/Earl Bathurst*	GWR 4073 Castle Class 4-6-0	Static	GWR Green
5227	GWR 5205 Class 2-8-0T	Static (Barry condition)	Primer
6106	GWR 6100 Class	Static	GWR Green

South East

Number(s) (Operating Number Highlighted)	Type	Status	Livery
6697	GWR 5600 Class 0-6-2T	Static	GWR Green
5322	GWR 4300 Class 2-6-0	Static	RoD Desert Sand
5572	GWR 5475 Class 2-6-2T	Static	GWR Green
7808 *Cookham Manor*	GWR 7800 Class Manor 4-6-0	Static	GWR Green
5900 *Hinderton Hall*	GWR 4900 Class Hall 4-6-0	Static	GWR Green
6998 *Burton Agnes Hall*	GWR 6959 Class Modified Hall 4-6-0	Static	GWR Green
6023 *King Edward II*	GWR 6000 Class King 4-6-0	Undergoing repair	BR Blue
7202	GWR 7200 Class 2-8-2T	Undergoing restoration	GWR Green
Steam Railmotor			
93	GWR 0-4-0	Static	Maroon
Broad Gauge Replicas			
Fire Fly	2-2-2	Static	Wood/Copper/Brass
Iron Duke	4-2-2	Static	Wood/Copper/Brass
New Build Steam Locos			
4709	GWR 4700 Class 2-8-0	Undergoing construction	TBC
1014 *County of Glamorgan*	GWR 1000 Class Grange 4-6-0	Undergoing construction	TBC
2999 *Lady of Legend*	GWR 2900 Class 4-6-0	Operational	GWR Green
Ex-Industrial Steam Locos			
7544 *Bonnie Prince Charlie*	RSH 0-4-0ST	Static	Blue
5 *Shannon/Jane*	George England 0-4-0WT	Static	Red
2409 *King George*	Hunslet 0-6-0ST	Undergoing overhaul	Red

GWR diesel railcar No 22 is seen working demonstration branch line services at the Didcot Railway Centre on 22 April 2011.

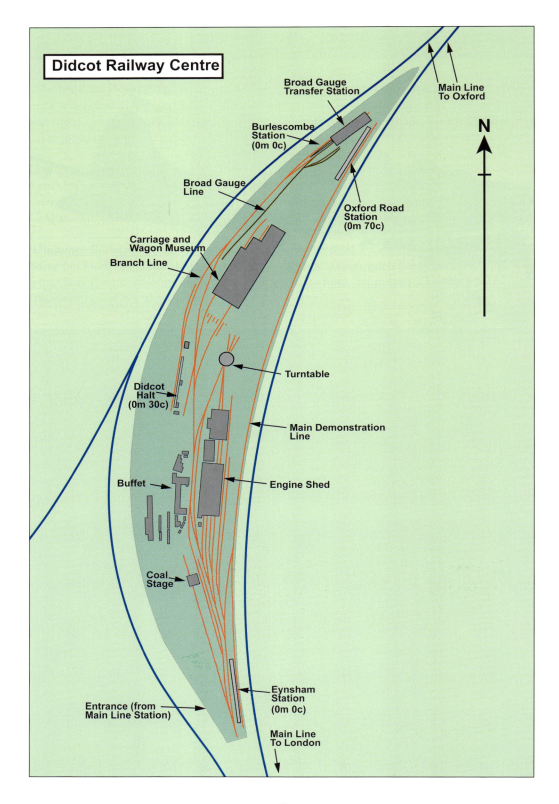

Kent and East Sussex Railway

The Kent and East Sussex Railway (K&ESR), originally known as the Rother Valley Railway, opened relatively late in 1900, following the Light Railways Act, which enabled lighter construction with lower speeds. It has a complicated history, being operated in two separate sections, Robertsbridge–Tenterden Town and Tenterden Town–Headcorn. Some through coaches originated at Cannon Street in connection with the hop-picking season. As one of Colonel Stephens' light railways, the line was never very profitable and was lucky to survive until 1961 under BR. The line reopened between Tenterden and Rolvenden as a heritage operation in 1974, extending to Bodiam in 2000. The 10½-mile line through the Rother Valley from Junction Road Halt through Bodiam to Tenterden is preserved as the KESR, with an additional short section from Robertsbridge operated by the Rother Valley Railway. The main operating base is at Tenterden, with main workshops and depot at Rolvenden. The K&ESR allocated two digit running numbers to all its locomotives and Diesel Multiple Units (see table).

Getting there: Bus links operate from Headcorn (12 and 12RL), Tunbridge Wells (297), Hastings (340), Maidstone (12) and Ashford International (2 and 2A). Car park at Tenterden – TN30 6LF.

Refreshments: Snacks from the refreshment kiosk at Tenterden. Pub: This Ancient Boro', Tenterden, 15 minutes' walk, guest beers and hot food.

Future plans: Longer term, the line is expected to be extended to join the Rother Valley Railway, giving a through run from Tenterden to Robertsbridge, although crossing the A21 main road near Robertsbridge will involve major civil engineering work. The Rother District Council granted planning permission in March 2017 for the KESR to extend from Junction Road to Northbridge Street.

Website: kesr.org.uk

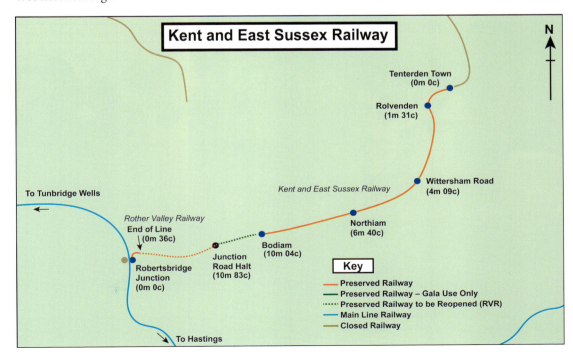

Number(s) (Operating Number Highlighted)	Type	Status	Livery
Ex-BR Diesel Locos			
D2023	Class 03	Operational	BR Green
D2024	Class 03	Awaiting overhaul	BR Green
3174 *Dover Castle* (08108)	Class 08	Awaiting overhaul	Black
D9504	Class 14	Under overhaul	BR Two-Tone Green
D9526	Class 14	Operational	BR Two-Tone Green
D7594 (25244)	Class 25	Awaiting restoration	BR Blue
Ex-Industrial Diesel Locos			
40 (16)	BTH Bo-Bo	Undergoing repair	Oxford Blue
41 (1)	Ruston and Hornsby 0-4-0DE	Operational	Dark Green
Diesel Multiple Units			
50971	Class 108 DMBS	Operational	BR Green
51571	Class 108 DMCL	Operational	BR Green
20	GWR Diesel Railcar	Undergoing restoration	GWR
Ex-BR Steam Locos			
32670 *Bodiam* (No 3)	LB&SCR A1 Class Terrier 0-6-0T	Undergoing overhaul	BR Lined Black
2678 *Knowle* (No 8)	LB&SCR A1 Class Terrier 0-6-0T	Operational	BR Lined Black
No 11 (753)	SECR P Class 0-6-0PT	Undergoing overhaul	SECR Blue
300 *Frank S Ross* (30070)	S100 Class (USA) 0-6-0T	Operational	LMR Blue
No 22 *Maunsell* (30065)	S100 Class (USA) 0-6-0T	Operational	SR Black
No 32 (6619)	GWR 5600 Class Pannier 0-6-0PT	Stored	BR Black
4253	GWR 4200 Class 2-8-0T	Undergoing restoration	TBC
Ex-Foreign Main Line Steam Locos			
No 19 *Norwegian* (376)	NSB 21c Class	Undergoing overhaul	NSB Black
Ex-Industrial Steam Locos			
No 12 *Marcia*	Peckett 1287 Class 0-4-0T	Awaiting repairs	Green
No 14 *Charwelton*	Manning Wardle Modified Class O	Undergoing overhaul	Brown
No 23 *Holman F Stephens*	Hunslet Austerity 0-6-0ST	Stored	Green
No 25 *Northiam*	Hunslet Austerity 0-6-0ST	Operational	Black

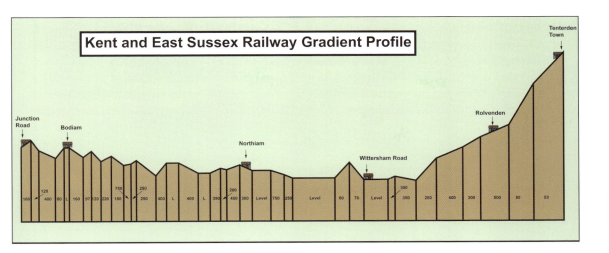

On 3 May 2009, 33052 with a heritage Victorian coach and 32670 *Bodiam* (No 3) at the rear roll down the bank between Tenterden and Rolvenden, the Terrier being dwarfed by the coach and the diesel loco. The Class 33 has since moved to the Bluebell Railway.

Spa Valley Railway

Originally opened by the London, Brighton and South Coast Railway (LB&SCR) in 1866, the Spa Valley Railway runs for 5½ miles from Tunbridge Wells West to Eridge, linking with the Oxted Line. The main depot, workshops and headquarters are at Tunbridge Wells West. The line was closed by BR in 1985, with the first one-mile section from Tunbridge Wells to High Rocks being reopened in 1997 and the opening through to Eridge completed in 2011.

Getting there: A cross-platform connection is available at Eridge with a 10-minute walk between stations at Tunbridge Wells for main line services. Car park at Eridge – TN3 LE.

Refreshments: Static buffet car *Emily* at Tunbridge Wells; snacks at Groombridge and Eridge. Pubs: The Sussex Arms, Tunbridge Wells, ten minutes' walk, guest beers; The Huntsman, Eridge, 2 minutes' walk, Hall & Woodhouse beers, hot food.

Future plans: Project East Grinstead would see a 9-mile extension from Eridge, crossing the Uckfield Line with a flyover at Ashurst Junction. DEMU 1317 has been earmarked for services on the route, with the possibility of the use of a new build Southern Railway 0-8-0 Z Class tank. This project appears to now be on the back burner.

Website: www.spavalleyrailway.co.uk

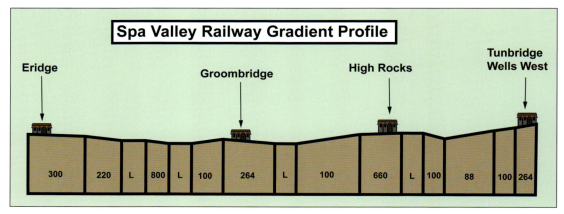

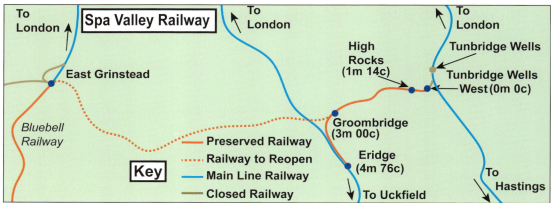

Number(s) (Operating Number Highlighted)	Type	Status	Livery
Ex-BR Diesel Locos			
09026	Class 09	Undergoing overhaul	Southern Green
D3489 *Colonel Tomline*	Class 10	Operational	BR Black
15224	Class 12	Stored	BR Green
31430 *Sister Dora*	Class 31	Operational	BR Blue
33063 *RJ Mitchell*	Class 33	Operational	Mainline Freight Triple Grey
33065	Class 33	Undergoing overhaul	Primer
73140	Class 73	Undergoing repair	Network SouthEast
Ex-Industrial Diesel Locos			
2591	Drewry 0-4-0	Operational	Black
Diesel Multiple Units			
54408 – DTCL	Class 101	Operational as hauled stock	BR Southern Green
51849 – DMBS	Class 115	Undergoing restoration	BR Green
Diesel Electric Multiple Units			
207017 (60142 + 60616 + 60916)	Class 207 DMBSO + TCL + DTSO	Operational	BR Blue/Grey
Electric Multiple Units			
1497 (76764 + 62402 + 76835)	Class 421 3-CIG DTCL + MBSO + DTCL	Used as hauled stock	BR Blue/Grey
9104 (68503)	Class 489 GLV	Stored	Gatwick Express
69306	Class 422 4-BIG TSRB	Static cafe	BR Green
Ex-BR Steam Locos			
68007	LNER J94 Austerity 0-6-0T	Undergoing overhaul	Black
650	LB&SCR Terrier 0-6-0T	Undergoing overhaul	LBSCR Green
47493	LMS Jinty 0-6-0T	Undergoing overhaul	BR Black
34053 *Sir Keith Park*	SR Battle of Britain Class 4-6-2	Operational	BR Lined Green
Ex-Industrial Steam Locos			
2890 *Douglas*	Hunslet Austerity 0-6-0	Operational	Black
1589 *Newstead*	Hunslet Austerity 0-6-0T	Undergoing overhaul	Blue
2315 *Lady Ingrid*	Andrew Barclay 0-4-0ST	Undergoing overhaul	Red
No 62 *Ugly*	RSH 0-6-0ST	Awaiting overhaul	Blue
57 *Samson*	RSH 0-6-0ST	Stored	Red
2193 *Topham*	Bagnall 0-6-0ST	Stored	Black

D8098 stands at Eridge on the evening of 1 August 2015 on an evening 'beerex', as part of the Spa Valley Railway's diesel gala.

Watercress Line/Mid-Hants Railway

The Mid-Hants Railway, marketed as the 'Watercress Line', runs 10 miles from Alton to New Alresford. It was opened in 1865 by the Alton, Alresford and Winchester Railway Company and taken over by the LSWR in 1884, then the Southern in 1923, being used as an alternative route between London and Southampton. The line was closed by BR in 1973 and sold in 1975. In its latter years, services were provided by Class 205 diesel electric multiple units (DEMUs). Alresford to Ropley was reopened in 1977, with the main shed and workshops established at the latter. The line was opened through to Medstead and Four Marks in 1983 and finally to Alton in 1985. The line is the only preserved railway with complete automatic warning system (AWS), used by locomotives and DEMUs. The AWS, and favourable alignments, enable high-speed rolling stock testing. Steep gradients are a feature of the line, with the climb out of Alresford at 1 in 80 rising up to 1 in 60 between Ropley and Medstead. Out of Alton, the line climbs up for 4 miles at 1 in 60; the crews refer to the climb up to Medstead (the highest station in southern England at 652ft) as going 'over the Alps'.

Getting there: Alton station is served by South West Railway with a 1 hour journey time and a half-hourly service pattern from London Waterloo (hourly on Sundays before midday). Stagecoach operates bus service 64 from Winchester to Alton and Velvet Bus operates number 67 from Winchester to Alresford. Cheap car parking at Alresford station – SO24 9JG.

Refreshments: Station buffet at Alresford, hot food and drinks. Pub: The Railway Arms (Triple fff Brewery), Alton, five minutes' walk, guest ales, no hot food.

Future plans: Extension from Alresford on to the former junction with the main line at Winchester Junction (2 miles north of Winchester) would require a bridge across the M3 and tunnelling under houses built on the former trackbed. It is unlikely to happen in the foreseeable future.

Website: watercressline.co.uk

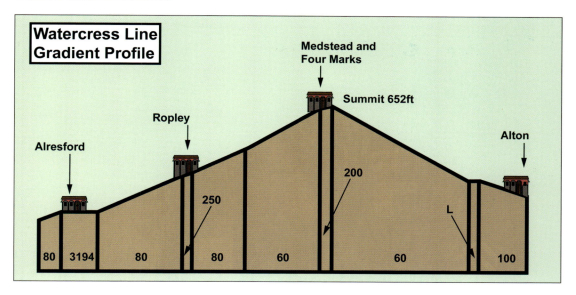

Number(s) (Operating Number Highlighted)	Type	Status	Livery
Ex-BR Diesel Locos			
08032 *Mendip*	Class 08	Stored	Foster Yeoman Blue
08288 *Phoenix*	Class 08	Operational	BR Blue
08377	Class 08	Undergoing repair	BR Green
12082	Class 11	Operational	BR Black
D8059 (20059)	Class 20	Operational	BR Green
D8188 (20188)	Class 20	Operational	BR Green
47579 *James Nightall G.C.*	Class 47	Awaiting repair	BR Stratford Large Logo
50027 *Lion*	Class 50	Operational	Network SouthEast
Diesel Electric Multiple Units			
202025 (60124 + 60824)	Class 205 DMBSO + DTCL	Body repairs	BR Green
Ex-BR Steam Locos			
828 *Harry A Frith*	LSWR S15 Class 4-6-0	Undergoing restoration	SR Olive Green
30499	LSWR S15 Class 4-6-0	Undergoing restoration	Primer
30506	LSWR S15 Class 4-6-0	Operational	SR Wartime Black
30850 *Lord Nelson*	SR Lord Nelson Class 4-6-0	Stored	BR Green
30925 *Cheltenham*	SR V Class Schools 4-6-0	Operational	BR Green
34007 *Wadebridge*	SR West Country Class 4-6-2	Stored	BR Lined Green
34058 *Sir Frederick Pile*	SR Battle of Britain Class 4-6-2	Stored	Primer
34105 *Swanage*	SR West Country Class 4-6-2	Undergoing overhaul	BR Lined Green
35005 *Canadian Pacific*	SR Merchant Navy Class 4-6-2	Undergoing overhaul	BR Lined Green
53808	S&DJR 7F 2-8-0	Operational	BR Unlined Black
41312	LMS Class 2MT 2-6-2T	Operational	BR Black
73096	BR Standard 5 4-6-0	Stored	BR Lined Green
75079	BR Standard 4 4-6-0	Undergoing restoration	Primer
76017	BR Standard 4 4-6-0	Operational	BR Black
80150	BR Standard 4MT 2-6-4T	Stored	BR Unlined Black
Ex-Industrial Steam Locos			
No 1 *Thomas* (3781)	Hunslet Austerity 0-6-0ST	Operational	'Thomas' Blue

South East

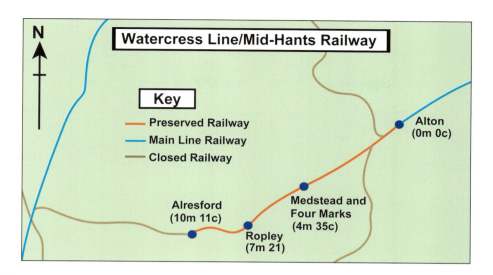

In September 2016, 9F 92212 stands at Medstead, Watercress Line.

Chapter 3

East of England

Colne Valley Railway

The Colne Valley Railway is based at Castle Hedingham station, near Halstead in Essex, and has a one-mile-long running line and a fully reconstructed station sited on part of the former Colne Valley and Halstead Railway (CVHR), which opened between 1860 and 1863. The railway is built on the section opened as a through line from Birdbrook to Wakes Colne, which closed in 1962.

Getting there: The closest railway station is Braintree (10 miles), and an hourly bus (number 89) runs from Braintree town centre and Great Yeldham, stopping outside the railway entrance, Monday to Friday. There is a less frequent service on Saturdays and no service on Sundays or Bank Holidays. Car Park – CO9 3DZ.

Refreshments: Clear Water Coffee, snacks and hot drinks; Station Buffet in two Mk.1 coaches, hot and cold food. Pub: several pubs in Castle Hedingham, no guest beers.

Future plans: On 6 December 2016, Colne Valley Railway Preservation Limited (CVRPL) announced that the railway was secured after the site was purchased from CVR Co Ltd following a heritage lottery fund grant for £1.75m, together with support from Braintree District Council. Track extensions are likely to take place in the near future.

Website: www.colnevalleyrailway.co.uk

Hunslet 0-6-0ST Austerity WD190 and train at Castle Headingham on the Colne Valley Railway. (PeterSkuce, CC BY-SA 4.0 <https://creativecommons.org/licenses/by-sa/4.0>, via Wikimedia Commons)

Number(s) (Operating Number Highlighted)	Type	Status	Livery
Ex-BR Diesel Locos			
D2041	Class 03	Operational	BR Green
D2184	Class 03	Operational	BR Black
43071	HST Power Car	Undergoing repair	First Group Blue
43073	HST Power Car	Undergoing repair	East Midlands Trains
43082	HST Power Car	Operational	East Midlands Trains
Ex-Industrial Diesel Locos			
4007	Hibberd 4wDM	Stored	Green
281266	Ruston and Hornsby 165DS	Operational	Blue
YD43	Ruston and Hornsby 0-4-0DM	Operational	Green
349/41	Andrew Barclay Sons and Co 0-4-0DM	Operational	BR Green
No 1 *Henry*	Fordson Major 4wd	Operational	Green
Diesel Multiple Units			
51339	Class 117 DMBS	Operational	BR Green
51382	Class 117 DMS	Operational	BR Green
55003	Class 121 DMBS	Operational	BR Green
Electric Multiple Units			
71205	Class 312 TSO	Stored	BR Blue
78037	Class 312 DTCOL	Stored	BR Blue
75023	Class 307 BDTBSO	Stored	BR Blue
75881	Class 308 BDTCOL	Undergoing restoration	Primer
Ex-BR Steam Locos			
45163	LMS Class 5MT Black 5 4-6-0	Undergoing restoration	Primer
45293	LMS Class 5MT Black 5 4-6-0	Undergoing restoration	Primer
35010 *Blue Star*	SR Merchant Navy Class 4-6-2	Undergoing restoration	Primer
Ex-Industrial Steam Locos			
WD190	Hunslet Austerity 0-6-0ST	Operational	Army Olive Green
WD200	Hunslet Austerity 0-6-0ST	Undergoing restoration	Black
60 *Jupiter*	RSH	Undergoing restoration	Blue
1875 *Barrington*	Avonside	Stored	Blue
No 1	Hawthorn Leslie Ltd.	Stored	Green

Epping Ongar Railway

The Epping Ongar Railway, the closest preserved line to London, is set in some of Essex's finest countryside, with steep gradients and unique station buildings, including the well-restored original Great Eastern station at Ongar. The line was originally a Great Eastern Railway (GER) branch and went on to form part of London Underground's (LU) Central Line extension from Liverpool Street to Ongar before closure in 1994. The line was bought in 1998 and reopened as a heritage railway in 2004, using a Class 117 DMU to provide a service between Coopersale and Ongar. After being sold on in 2007, the line was reborn as a steam and diesel heritage operation in May 2012. Since then, trains have operated on Saturdays, Sundays, Bank Holidays and selected school holiday weekdays, with a wide range of special events throughout the year. The main headquarters and maintenance base is in North Weald, where the station has been restored to 1940s condition. The railway features London Transport kilometre distance posts, with all distances on the Central Line still measured from Ongar; the 0.0km post is mounted by the bufferstop there.

Getting there: From London Underground, the railway operates vintage buses on route 339 from outside Epping Underground station on most operating days. These connect Epping Underground and Shenfield main line stations to Ongar and North Weald. Route 339 operates between Epping and North Weald via the B181 (Epping Road), with some services carrying on to Ongar, terminating outside The Two Brewers pub. The railway also runs bus services on to Shenfield station via Brentwood High Street, and passengers can also board and alight from all bus stops along the way.

Refreshments: Anglia Café, North Weald station; Buffet Shop café, Ongar station. Pub: The Cock Pub & Kitchen, Ongar, 10 minutes' walk, three guest beers, hot food.

Future plans: The owner intends to extend trains to a new platform at Epping Glade, near the LU station. A halt at Coopersale is under consideration, together with further siding space at North Weald for additional stock.

Website: https://www.eorailway.co.uk

D6729 (37029) approaches North Weald on a train from Ongar to Coopersale on 23 April 2016.

Number(s) (Operating Number Highlighted)	Type	Status	Livery
Ex-BR Diesel Locos			
03119	Class 03	Stored	BR Blue
D2170 (**03170**)	Class 03	Operational	BR Green
D8001 (**20001**)	Class 20	Operational	BR Green
31438	Class 31	Operational	BR Blue
D6729 (**37029**)	Class 37	Operational	BR Green
45132	Class 45	Heavy overhaul	BR Blue
47635 *Jimmy Milne*	Class 47	Operational	BR Large Logo Blue
Ex-Industrial Diesel Locos			
RH398616	Ruston and Hornsby 0-4-0	Plinthed at Ongar	Non-standard Brown
Diesel Multiple Units			
51342	Class 117 DMBS	Undergoing restoration	Primer
51384	Class 117 DMS	Operational	BR Green
56287	Class 121 DTS	Operational	BR Green
Diesel Electric Multiple Units			
205205 (60110 + 60810)	Class 205 DMBSO + DTSOL	In use as hauled stock	Network SouthEast
Electric Multiple Units			
DM 1031	1959 Tube Stock	Static	London Transport Red
70235	Class 411 4-CEP TBCK	Undergoing restoration	Primer
69345	Class 412 4-BEP TRSB	Undergoing restoration	Primer
Ex-BR Steam Locos			
4141	GWR 5101 Class Large Prairie	Undergoing overhaul	BR Green
4953 *Pitchford Hall*	4900 Class Hall 4-6-0	Operational	BR Lined Black
4141	5101 Class Large Prairie	Undergoing overhaul	BR Green
Ex-Industrial Steam Locos			
3437 *Isabel*	Hawthorn Leslie 0-6-0ST	Operational	NCB Red
3837 (S&L 16)	Hawthorn Leslie	Awaiting restoration	Blue
S&L 56 (7667)	RSH 0-6-0ST	Stored	Black
S&L 63 (7761)	RSH 0-6-0ST	Stored	Blue

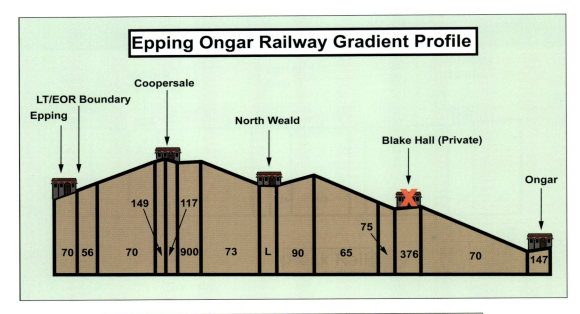

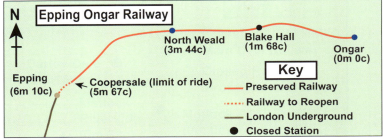

At the London Transport Gala, over the weekend of 9–10 October 2021, LT-liveried L150 (4575 Class 2-6-2T) number 5521 heads a train for Ongar at North Weald. Pannier tank L92 has just dropped off the rear of the train.

Mid-Norfolk Railway

Part of the former Great Eastern line from Wymondham to Wells-next-the-Sea, the section from Wymondham to Dereham was reopened in May 1999. The line is now used as far north as Worthing for training and possibly on special operating days.

Getting there: The MNR station at Wymondham is a short walk from the main line station. Buses also run from Norwich and King's Lynn. Free car parking at Dereham – NR19 1DF.

Refreshments: Hot meals and snacks at the buffet on the platform at Dereham. Pub: Railway Tavern, Dereham, 10 minutes' walk, guest beers, hot food.

Future plans: North of County School, the line extended to Fakenham and originally connected with the current Wells and Walsingham Railway. Reconnecting the lines would be a very long-term proposition. Reopening to Fakenham remains the main objective.

Website: www.midnorfolkrailway.co.uk

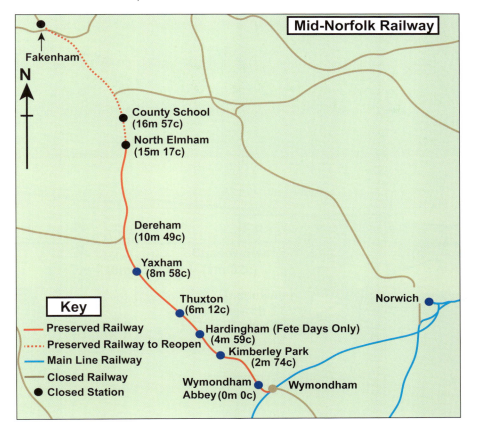

Number(s) (Operating Number Highlighted)	Type	Status	Livery
Ex-BR Diesel Locos			
03197	Class 03	Operational	BR Blue
D2334	Class 04	Undergoing repair	BR Green
D9520	Class 14	Operational	BR Two-Tone Green
31255	Class 31	Undergoing restoration	EWS Maroon/Gold
33202 *Dennis G. Robinson*	Class 33	Operational	BR Blue
47367 *Kenny Cockbird*	Class 47	Operational	BR Blue
47580 *County of Essex*	Class 47	Operational	BR Blue with Union Flag
D1933 *Aldeburgh Festival* (47596)	Class 47	Operational	BR Two-Tone Green
50019 *Ramillies*	Class 50	Undergoing overhaul	BR Large Logo Blue
Ex-Industrial Diesel Locos			
D1049 (BSC1)	English Electric 0-6-0DH	Operational	BSC Yellow
Diesel Multiple Units			
56301	Class 100 DTCL	Static display	BR Green
51226	Class 101 DMBS	Undergoing repair	BR Green
51499	Class 101 DMCL	Undergoing repair	BR Green
51434	Class 101 DMBC	Operational	BR Blue/Grey
51503	Class 101 DMCL	Operational	BR Blue/Grey
56347	Class 101 DTCL	Operational	BR Green
59117	Class 101 TCL	Stored	BR Blue/Grey
51942	Class 108 DMBS	Stored	Network SouthEast
54270	Class 108 DTCL	Stored	Network SouthEast
51370	Class 117 DMBS	Undergoing restoration	BR Green
51412	Class 117 DMS	Undergoing restoration	BR Green
142038 (55579 + 55629)	Class 142 DMS + DMSL	Operational	Northern Rail
142061 (55711 + 55757)	Class 142 DMS + DMSL	Operational	Northern Rail
144018 (55818 + 55854 + 55841)	Class 144 DMS + MS + DMSL	Operational	Northern Rail
Electric Multiple Units			
68004	Class 419 MLV	Stored	BR Green
Ex-BR Steam Locos			
80078	BR Standard 4 2-6-4T	Operational	BR Lined Black

East of England

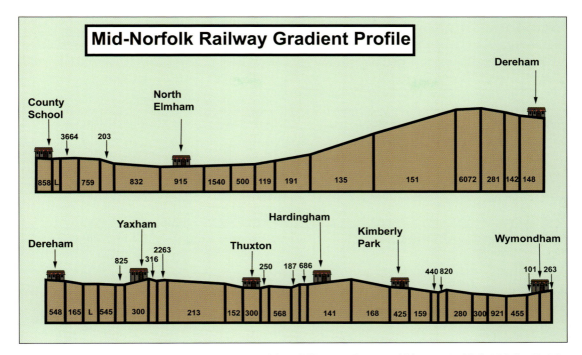

On 18 March 2011, Class 37s 37003, in Civil Engineer's 'Dutch' livery, and 37219 *Shirley Ann Smith*, in Mainline Freight blue, approach Dereham with a train from Wymondham during the annual diesel gala at the Mid-Norfolk Railway.

Nene Valley Railway

The line runs from Yarwell Junction, where lines diverted to Rugby and Northampton, to Peterborough. A lack of suitable British locos and the availability of a Swedish loco (S1 Class 2-6-4T 1928) saw the line reopen to continental loading gauge in 1977, and it has been used for much filming work, including movies. The main depot and workshops are at Wansford.

Getting there: Buses run from Peterborough to Orton Mere and Ferry Meadows. Peterborough is a short walk from the main line station. Free parking at Wansford – PE8 6LR.

Refreshments: Full buffet at Wansford, hot food and drinks. Pubs: Charters, a floating converted Dutch grain barge on the River Nene, 10 minutes' walk from Peterborough Nene Valley station, guest beers, hot food.

Future plans: The proposed 'Crescent Link' would involve running into the main line station at Peterborough and possibly extending the line over a mile eastward to the old Peterborough East station.

Website: www.nvr.org.uk

Number(s) (Operating Number Highlighted)	Type	Status	Livery
Ex-BR Diesel Locos			
9529	Class 14	Operational	BR Blue
45041 *Royal Tank Regiment*	Class 45	Operational	BR Blue
Ex-Industrial Diesel Locos			
10202 *Barabell*	Sentinel 4wDM	Operational	Blue
DL83	Sentinel 0-6-0DH	Operational	London Transport Green
2896 *Frank*	Hibberd 0-4-0	Undergoing restoration	Blue
D2654	Yorkshire	Undergoing repair	Green
1123	English Electric 0-4-0	Undergoing overhaul	Grey
304469	Ruston and Hornsby 0-4-0	Stored	Green
Diesel Multiple Units			
143602 (55651 + 55668)	Class 143 DMS + DMSL	Operational	Arriva Trains Wales
1212 *Helga*	SJ Y7 Railcar	Operational	SJ Orange
Ex-BR Steam Locos			
34081 *92 Squadron*	SR Battle of Britain Class	Operational	SR Green
73050 *City of Peterborough*	BR Standard Class 5 4-6-0	Undergoing overhaul	BR Lined Black
Ex-Industrial Steam Locos			
1800 *Thomas*	Hudswell Clarke 0-6-0T	Operational	Thomas Blue
75006	Hunslet Austerity 0-6-0ST	Awaiting overhaul	Brown
1953 *Jacks Green*	Hunslet 0-6-0ST	Static	Red
1539 *Derek Crouch*	Hudswell Clarke 0-6-0ST	Undergoing overhaul	Maroon
1626 *Toby*	Cockerill 0-4-0WT Tram Engine	Stored	Primer

East of England

Number(s) (Operating Number Highlighted)	Type	Status	Livery
Ex-Foreign Steam Locos			
656 *Tinkerbell*	Danish DSB Class F 0-6-0T	Undergoing overhaul	Black
1178	SJ Swedish Class S 2-6-2T	Awaiting overhaul	Blue
101	Swedish SJ B Class 4-6-0	Static	Blue
5485	PKP Class TKp/Slask 0-8-0T	Operational	Green
64 305	DB Class 64 2-6-2T	Stored	Black

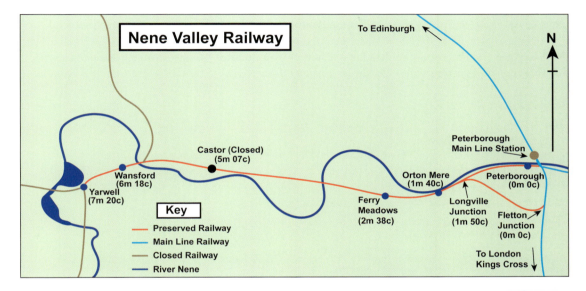

55022 *Royal Scots Grey*, running in disguise as 55018 *Ballymoss*, nears Ferry Meadows on 9 April 2017, with a train from Wansford to Peterborough. Deltics often appear as high-profile guests for diesel galas at many preserved railways.

North Norfolk Railway

The 5¼-mile-long line from Sheringham to Holt passes over unexpectedly steep gradients with sea views to the north. Opened in 1887, as part of the Midland and Great Northern Joint Railway, the line was closed in 1964, with a new station built at Sheringham to retain the main line connection to Norwich. The line was reopened in 1975, with the main depot at Weybourne and a carriage shed at Holt. In 2010, the NNR was reconnected to the national rail network at Sheringham after reinstatement of the level crossing at Sheringham East. The railway operates summer dining specials over the main line to Cromer.

Getting there: Sheringham is served by Greater Anglia direct from Norwich and Sanders Coaches numbers 44, X44 and 44A between Sheringham, Cromer, Aylsham and on to Norwich via Hainford and Horsham St Faith. Sanders also operates Coasthopper services linking Sheringham, Wells-next-the-Sea, Hunstanton, King's Lynn, Cromer and Norwich. Holt is also served by Sanders – numbers 4, 5 and 9. Car parking at Holt by donation – NR25 6AJ.

Refreshments: Old luggage office on platform at Sheringham, snacks and drinks; buffets at Holt and Weybourne. Pub: The Ship Inn, Weybourne, 20 minutes' walk, local guest beers, hot food.

Future plans: The Norfolk Orbital Line is a long-term project, independent of the North Norfolk Railway, although the line would be included. The aim is to link Sheringham and Wymondham, joining Network Rail at both ends. Some trackbed has been purchased and some earthworks completed, with an extension nearer to Holt (Centre) the first step.

Website: www.nnrailway.co.uk

On 14 June 2014, Class 14 diesel hydraulic D9531 *Ernest* waits to depart from Holt on the North Norfolk Railway with a service for Sheringham, with D6732 (37032) on the rear.

Number(s) (Operating Number Highlighted)	Type	Status	Livery
Ex-BR Diesel Locos			
D2051 (**03051**)	Class 03	Stored	Grey
D2063 (**03063**)	Class 03	Undergoing overhaul	BR Blue
D3935 (**08767**)	Class 08	Operational	BR Green
D3940 (**08772**)	Class 08	Undergoing overhaul	BR Green
12131	Class 11	Operational	Black
20227 *Sherlock Holmes*	Class 20	Operational	London Transport Maroon
D5631 (**31207**)	Class 31	Operational	BR Green
D6732 (**37032**)	Class 37	Operational	BR Green
Diesel Multiple Units			
51188	Class 101 DMBS	Operational	BR Green
56352	Class 101 DTCL	Operational	BR Green
51228	Class 101 DMBS	Operational	BR Green
56062	Class 101 DTCL	Operational	BR Green
51192	Class 101 DMBS	Stored	BR Green
50479	Class 104 DMBS	Undergoing restoration	BR Green
56182	Class 104 DTCL	Undergoing restoration	BR Blue
79960	Waggon and Maschinenbau Railbus	Operational	BR Green
Ex-BR Steam Locos			
1744	GNR Class N2 0-6-2T	Undergoing overhaul	Primer
564	GER Class Y14 0-6-0	Operational	GER Lined Blue
8572	LNER Class B12 4-6-0	Awaiting overhaul	LNER Apple Green
53809	S&DJR Class 7F 2-8-0	Operational	BR Unlined Black
76084	BR Standard Class 4 2-6-0	Operational	BR Lined Black
92203 *Black Prince*	BR Standard 9F 2-10-0	Operational	BR Unlined Black
90775 *The Royal Norfolk Regiment*	WD Austerity 2-10-0	Operational	BR Unlined Black
Ex Industrial Steam Locos			
1982 *Ring Haw*	Hunslet 0-6-0ST	Awaiting overhaul	Lined Green
1700 *Wissington*	Hudswell Clarke 0-6-0ST	Undergoing overhaul	Green

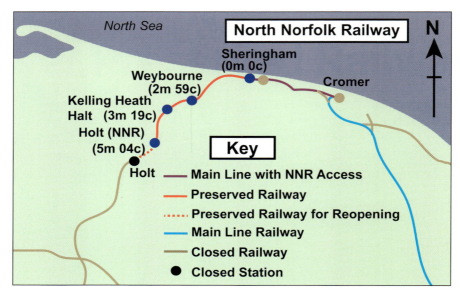

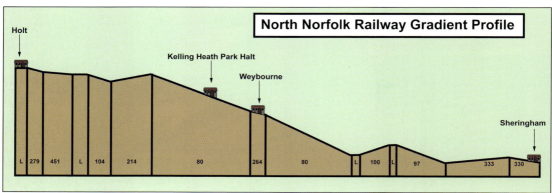

Chapter 4
East Midlands

Barrow Hill Roundhouse

Barrow Hill Roundhouse is sited just off the 'Old Road' freight line from Chesterfield to Rotherham Masborough, which was opened by the North Midland Railway in 1841 and absorbed by MR in 1866. The roundhouse, the last surviving example in Britain, was built by MR in 1870 and remained in use until 1991. Saved from demolition by Chesterfield Local Authority, it was reopened to the public in 1998. Up to 24 locos can be housed inside, with more in additional cover and sidings. Locos on-site can vary greatly, with many main line and preserved locos moving in and out after contract repairs. Access is available from the main line and a demonstration running line uses around a quarter mile of track, with trains hauled in top and tail mode.

Getting there: Stagecoach number 90 buses run from Chesterfield (New Beetwell Street) to Barrow Hill every 30 minutes from 06.40 to 17.40 Monday to Friday and 07.10 to 17.40 on Saturdays. A Sunday service is operated by TM Travel. There is generally a free bus service from Chesterfield main line station on gala days. By car, the postcode is S43 2PR.

Refreshments: Hot food and drinks in on-site buffet; annual beer festival on-site.

Future plans: There are no current plans for expansion of the available running line.

Website: www.barrowhill.org

On 16 October 2005, 20096 brings a shuttle service into the platform, tailed by D5528 (31110), with 47847 ready to replace the Class 31.

Number(s) (Operating Number Highlighted)	Type	Status	Livery
Ex-BR Diesel Locos			
D2853 (02003)	Class 02	For repairs	BR Green
D8268	Class 02	Operational	BR Green
03066	Class 03	Operational	BR Blue
07012	Class 07	Operational	BR Blue
D4092	Class 10	Operational	BR Green
26007	Class 26	Operational	Railfreight Red Stripe
27066	Class 27	Undergoing overhaul	BR Blue
45060 *Sherwood Forester*	Class 45	Operational	BR Blue
45105	Class 45	Undergoing restoration	BR Blue
45118	Class 45	Undergoing repair	BR Blue
55009 *Alycidon*	Class 55	Undergoing repair	BR Blue
D9015 (55015)	Class 55	Undergoing overhaul	BR Green
55019 *Royal Highland Fusilier*	Class 55	Operational	BR Blue
New Build			
D5910	Class 23	Construction	Primer
Ex-BR Electric Locos			
81002	Class 81	Stored	BR Blue
82008	Class 82	Stored	InterCity Executive
E3035 (83012)	Class 83	Stored	BR Electric Blue
85101	Class 85	Stored	BR Blue
89001 *Avocet*	Class 89	Undergoing repair	InterCity Swallow
Ex-Industrial Diesel Locos			
12589	Robert Stephens and Hawthorns 0-4-0DM0	Operational	Yellow
L149	EE 0-6-0	Operational	Yellow
Ex-Main Line Steam Locos			
506	GCR Director Class 11F 4-4-0	Static	GCR Blue
1000	Midland Compound 4-4-0	Static	LMS Maroon
8217	Holden J17 0-6-0	Static	LNER Black
41708	Midland Railway 0-6-0T	Awaiting overhaul	LMS Black
5164	GWR 5101 Class 2-6-2T	Static	GWR Green
Ex-Industrial Steam Locos			
2491	Hawthorn Leslie 0-4-0ST	Static	Blue
1795	Manning Wardle 0-4-0ST	Restoration	Black
WD75141	Hunslet 0-6-0ST	Restoration	Blue
2000	Peckett and Sons 0-6-0ST	Stored	Blue
68006	Hunslet 0-6-0ST	Restoration	Black
3272	Vulcan Foundry 0-4-0ST	Awaiting overhaul	Black

Battlefield Line

The line, opened in 1873 as part of the Ashby and Nuneaton Joint Railway between Nuneaton, Coalville and on to the Leicester to Burton line, operates over 4¾ miles from Shackerstone to Shenton. The line was closed by British Rail (BR) in 1965, partially reopening in 1973 as a preserved operation.

Getting there: Accessible by Roberts' number 7 bus to Shackerstone from Measham to Fenny Drayton via Atherstone main line rail station. Services to Market Bosworth run from Leicester (Arriva's 153) and Hinckley (Roberts' number 159). Free car parking at Shackerstone – CV13 0BS, paid car park at Shenton – CV13 6DJ.

Refreshments: Victorian tearoom in the station at Shackerstone, hot snacks and drinks. Pub: Rising Sun, Shackerstone, 15 minutes' walk, two guest beers, hot food.

Future plans: It is thought that plans to extend north to Coalville to connect with Snibston Discovery Park are no longer being considered.

Website: www.battlefieldline.co.uk

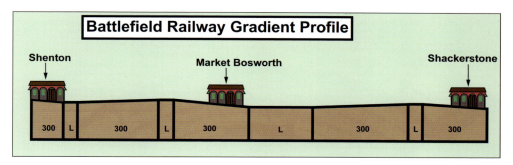

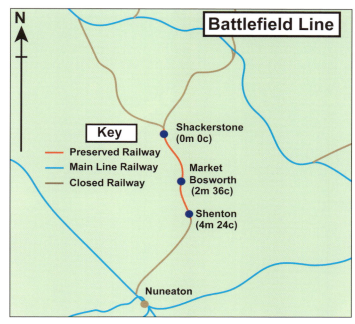

Number(s) (Operating Number Highlighted)	Type	Status	Livery
Ex-BR Diesel Locos			
D2867	Class 02	Operational	BR Green
D2310	Class 04	Operational	BR Green
12083	Class 11	Awaiting restoration	Black and Grey
CFD 2002 (20063)	Class 20	Awaiting restoration	CFD Orange/White
20087	Class 20	Awaiting repair	BR Blue/Red Stripe
D8110 (20110)	Class 20	Operational	BR Green
D7523 (25173)	Class 25	Heavy overhaul	BR Two-Tone Green
D6508 *Eastleigh* (33008)	Class 33	Undergoing repair	BR Green
33201	Class 33	Operational	BR Blue
D6593 (33208)	Class 33	Awaiting restoration	BR Green
37906	Class 37	Undergoing overhaul	Railfreight Original Grey
45015	Class 45	Awaiting scrapping	BR Blue
47640 *University of Strathclyde*	Class 47	Awaiting repair	BR Large Logo Blue
58048	Class 58	Undergoing restoration	EWS Maroon/Gold
Ex-Industrial Diesel Locos			
9921 *Rusty*	4wDM	Stored	Red
1901 *Davy*	English Electric 0-6-0DE	Awaiting overhaul	Green
No 2 *Nancy*	Ruston Hornsby 0-4-0	Stored	Dark Blue
242915 *Hercules*	Ruston Hornsby 0-4-0	Undergoing overhaul	Yellow and Pink
268881 *Mazda*	Ruston Hornsby 0-4-0DE	Operational	Green
594 *Big Momma*	Barclay 0-6-0	Stored	Light Green
422 *Hot Wheels*	Barclay 0-6-0	Stored	Blue
Electric Locos			
Spondon Power Station No 1 (E905)	English Electric 4wD	Operational (battery)	Green
Diesel Multiple Units			
51131	Class 116 DMBS	Operational	BR Blue/Grey
51321	Class 118 DMS	Undergoing repair	BR Blue/Grey
55005	Class 122 DMBS	Operational	BR Blue/Grey
Electric Multiple Units			
6291 (65321 + 77112)	Class 416 2-EPB DMBS + DTS	Awaiting restoration	Primer & BR Blue/Grey
Ex-Industrial Steam Locos			
Sir Gomer	Peckett Class OX1 0-6-0ST	Awaiting overhaul	Blue

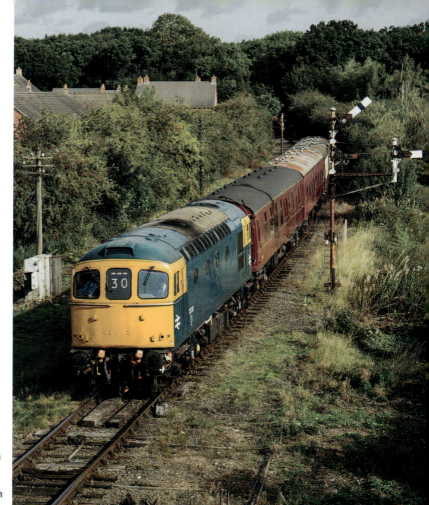

Right: On 12 September 2020, recently repainted 33201 approaches Market Bosworth with a Shackerstone to Shenton service.

Below: On 5 August 2007, one-time resident Class 73, 73114, stands at Shenton, the southern terminus of the Battlefield Line, with a train from Shackerstone. This loco is now technically de-preserved, being owned by Nemesis Rail at Burton upon Trent.

Ecclesbourne Valley Railway

Opened by the Midland Railway in 1867 and closed to passengers in 1947, the nine-mile-long branch from Duffield to Wirksworth remained open for infrequent limestone freight traffic until 1989. The headquarters and main workshops of the railway are based at Wirksworth station, with services operated in both directions between Wirksworth and Duffield and from Wirksworth to Ravenstor. The line reopened on 24 August 2004 with a half-mile section from Wirksworth to Gorsey Bank, then to Idridgehay and finally to Duffield in 2011. The ½-mile long 1 in 30 incline from Wirksworth to Ravenstor opened in 2005, giving access for visitors to the High Peak Trail.

Getting there: Since 2011, there are main line cross-platform connections with Matlock line trains at Duffield, with through ticketing available on to the branch. Buses also run from Derby to Wirksworth. Wirksworth has a large free car park – DE4 4FB.

Refreshments: The Station Café at Wirksworth provides hot food. Pub: Red Lion, Wirksworth, 5 minutes' walk, guest beers and hot food.

Future plans: With the whole branch now in use, there is no scope for route expansion.

Website: www.e-v-r.com

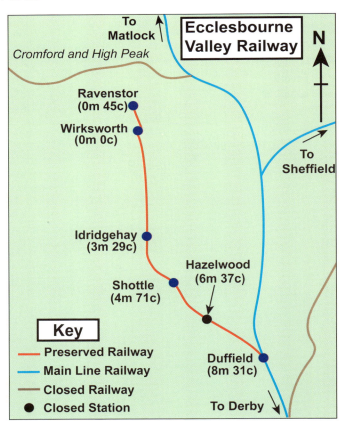

Number(s) (Operating Number Highlighted)	Type	Status	Livery
Ex-BR Diesel Locos			
D9537	Class 14	Operational	Black
31601 *Devon Diesel Society*	Class 31	Operational	DCR Grey
33103 *Swordfish*	Class 33	Operational	Departmental Grey
D1842 (47192)	Class 47	Operational	BR Two-Tone Green
58022	Class 58	Spares donor	Mainline Triple Grey
73210 *Selhurst*	Class 73	Awaiting repair	InterCity Swallow
Ex-Industrial Diesel Locos			
10275 *LJ Breeze*	Rolls Royce Steelman	Operational	Black
402803 *Faraday*	R and H 165DS Class	Undergoing restoration	Dark Green
319284 (11520)	R and H 165DS Class	Stored	Dark Green
9597 *Tom*	Thomas Hill Class 188c 4wDH	Operational	Blue
103c *Megan*	Thomas Hill Class 188c 4wDH	Awaiting repair	Blue
Diesel Multiple Units			
79018	Derby Lightweight DMBS	Undergoing restoration	Primer
79612	Derby Lightweight DTCL	Undergoing restoration	BR Blue
79900	Derby Lightweight DMBS Single Car	Operational	BR Green
50170	Class 101 DMCL	Operational	BR Green
59303	Class 101 TSL	Operational	BR Green
50253	Class 101 DMBS	Operational	BR Green
51505	Class 101 DMCL	Operational	BR Blue
53599	Class 108 DMBS	Operational	BR Blue/Grey
51567	Class 108 DMCL	Awaiting restoration	BR Blue/Grey
51073	Class 119 DMBC	Operational	BR Blue/Grey
977975 (55027)	Class 121 DMBS	Awaiting restoration	Primer
977976 (55031)	Class 121 DMBS	Stored	Network Rail Yellow
55006	Class 122 DMBS	Operational	BR Green
Electric Multiple Units			
8202 (72501 + 72617)	Class 488 TFOLH + TSOLH	Operational as hauled stock	Chocolate and Cream
9101 (68500)	Class 489 GLV	Static museum	Gatwick Express
9107 (68506)	Class 489 GLV	Operational as hauled stock	Chocolate and Cream
Ex-BR Steam Locos			
9466	GWR 9400 Class 0-6-0PT	Operational	GWR Green
80080	BR Standard Class 4MT 2-6-4T	Operational	BR Lined Black
Ex-Industrial Steam Locos			
2360 *Brian Harrison*	Andrew Barclay 0-4-0T	Undergoing overhaul	Green
2217 *Henry Ellison*	Andrew Barclay 0-4-0T	Operational	Blue
102 (1884) *Cathryn*	Hudswell Clarke 0-6-0T	Undergoing restoration	Blue
2746 *The Duke*	Bagnall Austerity 0-6-0T	Undergoing overhaul	Black

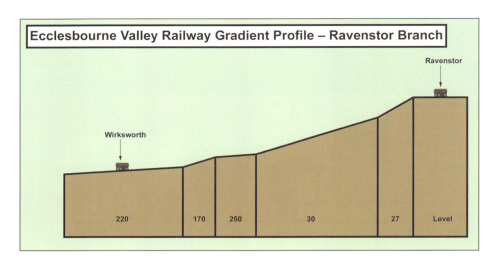

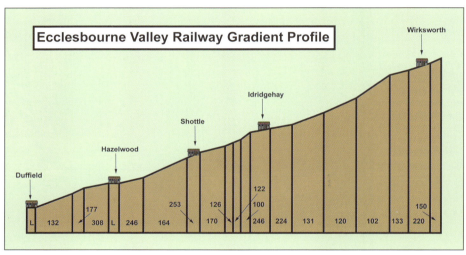

D7629 (25279) stands at Wirksworth on 6 August 2016 heading to Duffield with a selection of Class 101 DMU vehicles as hauled stock, and providing a service on the Ravenstor branch.

Great Central Railway

The Grand Central Railway (GCR), named after the original company that opened the route in 1897, runs from Leicester to Loughborough and is the UK's only preserved double-track main line railway. The main line was closed in 1969 between Nottingham and London Marylebone before partial reopening as a preserved operation in 1974. The main depot and workshops are based at Loughborough.

Getting there: Main line services to Loughborough and an approximate 15-minute walk to the GCR station. Arriva's 127 bus operates from Leicester to Shepshed, passing Rothley, Quorn and Loughborough. Free roadside parking at Loughborough – LE11 1RW, small free car park at Leicester North – LE4 3BR, and main cark park at Quorn – LE12 8BP.

Refreshments: Buffet serving hot food on platform at Loughborough; snacks in buffet at Leicester North. Pub: The Organ Grinder (Blue Monkey Brewery), Loughborough, 10 minutes' walk, Blue Monkey beers, no food.

Future plans: 'The Gap', a section of missing bridges and embankments, including one over the Midland Main Line, needs to be reinstated to join the GCR with the GCR(N) to enable through running between Leicester and Nottingham (Ruddington). The main bridge beams are now in place and through running is hoped to begin in the next few years. The Mountsorrel branch running from Rothley Sidings is now open and used on special days.

Website: www.gcrailway.co.uk

Number(s) (Operating Number Highlighted)	Type	Status	Livery
Ex-BR Diesel Locos			
07005	Class 07	Undergoing restoration	BR Green
D4137 (08907)	Class 08	Operational	BR Green
13101 (D3101)	Class 08	Operational	BR Green
10119 *Margaret Ethel-Thomas Alfred Naylor* (D4067)	Class 10	Operational	BR Blue
D8098 (20098)	Class 20	Operational	BR Green
D5185 (25035)	Class 25	Operational	BR Green
D5401 (27056)	Class 27	Undergoing restoration	BR Green
33116	Class 33	Operational	BR Blue
37714 *Cardiff Canton*	Class 37	Operational	Railfreight Metals
D123 *Leicestershire and Derbyshire Yeomanry* (45125)	Class 45	Operational	BR Green
1705 *Sparrowhawk* (47117)	Class 47	Awaiting repairs	BR Blue
50017 *Royal Oak*	Class 50	Operational	Network SouthEast

Number(s) (Operating Number Highlighted)	Type	Status	Livery
Ex-Industrial Diesel Locos			
393304	Ruston and Hornsby 48DS 0-4-0DM	Operational	Green
D4279	John Fowler 0-4-0DM	Stored	Dark Blue
Diesel Multiple Units			
50193	Class 101 DMCL	Stored	BR Blue/Grey
50203	Class 101 DMBS	Operational	BR Blue
50266	Class 101 DMCL	Operational	BR Blue
50321	Class 101 DMCL	Operational	BR Green
51427	Class 101 DMBS	Operational	BR Green
56342	Class 101 DTCL	Operational	BR Green
51396	Class 117 DMS	Stored	Network SouthEast
59506	Class 117 TCL	Operational	BR Blue
59575	Class 111 TSBL	Operational	BR Green
59276	Class 120 TSLRB	Stored	BR Green
55009	Class 122 DMBS	Undergoing restoration	BR Green
Electric Multiple Units			
70576	Class 411 4-CEP TBCK	Stored	BR Carmine/Cream
Ex-BR Steam Locos			
6990 *Witherslack Hall*	GWR Modified Hall 4-6-0	Operational	GWR Green
63601	GCR 8K Class 2-8-0	Awaiting overhaul	
777 *Sir Lamiel*	SR King Arthur Class 4-6-0	Awaiting overhaul	
34039 *Boscastle*	SR West Country 4-6-2	Undergoing overhaul	
47406	Jinty 0-6-0	Awaiting overhaul	LMS Black
46521	LMS Class 2-6-0	Operational	BR Lined Black
45305	LMS Class 5MT Black 5 4-6-0	Awaiting overhaul	BR Black
45491	LMS Class 5MT Black 5 4-6-0	Undergoing restoration	Primer
48305	LMS 8F 2-8-0	Operational	BR Black
48624	LMS 8F 2-8-0	Awaiting overhaul	LMS Maroon
78018	BR Standard Class 2 2-6-0	Operational	BR Lined Black
78019	BR Standard Class 2 2-6-0	Undergoing overhaul	BR Lined Black
73156	BR Standard 5 4-6-0	Operational	BR Lined Black
70013 *Oliver Cromwell*	BR Standard Britannia	Awaiting overhaul	BR Lined Green
92214 *City of Leicester*	BR Standard 9F 2-10-0	Operational	BR Green
Ex-Industrial Steam Locos			
68067	Hudswell Clarke Austerity 0-6-0ST	Operational	BR Black
3809	Hunslet Austerity 0-6-0ST	Undergoing restoration	BR Lined Black
7684 (Nechells No 4)	RSH Austerity 0-6-0T	Undergoing overhaul	Lined Green
Neepsend No 2	Sentinel 4wVBT	Awaiting restoration	Primer

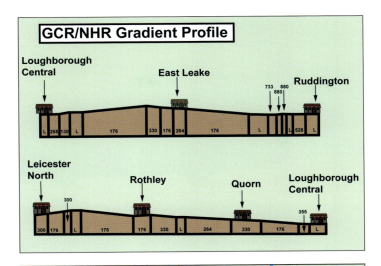
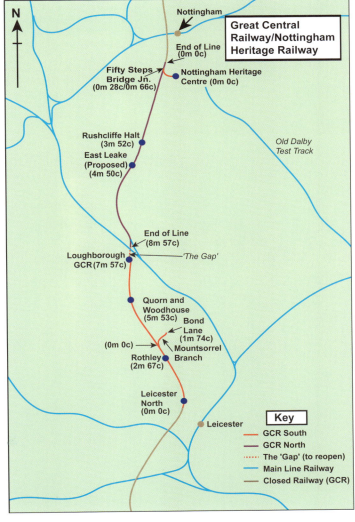

Above left: 55019 *Royal Highland Fusilier* stands at Leicester North on the evening of 18 September 2018 with a Saturday night beer special, as part of the GCR diesel gala.

Above right: GWR 2884 Class 2-8-0 3802, visiting from the Llangollen Railway, approaches Quorn on a special demonstration freight, hauling the GCR's rake of 'Windcutter' 16-ton mineral wagons on 1 October 2021.

Left: Class 3F Jinty tank 47406 passes Kinchley Lane on 13 April 2019.

Below: GWR Hall 6990 *Foremarke Hall* passes Kinchley Lane, a favourite spot for photographers on the GCR, on 2 February 2019.

Midland Railway – Butterley

Set in a 57-acre museum site and 35-acre country park, the Midland Railway Centre hosts a wide range of facilities and locomotives with a 3½-mile long running line and regular timetabled services. The original Midland Railway branch line from Derby to Butterley via Denby was primarily used for freight traffic, although a suburban passenger service was operated. The line from Butterley ran east to west from Ambergate to Ironville, connecting the two lines radiating south from Chesterfield to Derby and Nottingham.

Getting there: 25 minutes on the bus (services 9.1 and 9.3 from Alfreton), 9.1 bus also from Derby. Car parking free at Butterley – DE5 3QZ.

Refreshments: Buffet with hot food at Swanwick Junction; hot snacks at Butterley.

Future plans: With the main line connected to the east and no development opportunities for reopening to the west, the current track length is the probable maximum.

Website: www.midlandrailway-butterley.co.uk

Number(s) (Operating Number Highlighted)	Type	Status	Livery
Ex-BR Diesel Locos			
D2858	Class 02	Static display	BR Green
D2138	Class 03	Undergoing overhaul	BR Green
08331	Class 08	Operational	RT Rail Black
08590 *Red Lion*	Class 08	Operational	BR Blue
12077	Class 11	Operational	BR Green
20048	Class 20	Operational	BR Blue
D7671 (**25321**)	Class 25	Awaiting repair	BR Green
31108	Class 31	Operational	Railfreight Original Grey
5581 (**31162**)	Class 31	Operational	BR Blue
31414	Class 31	Undergoing restoration	Primer
31418	Class 31	Stored	Primer
40012	Class 40	Undergoing repair	BR Blue
43048	HST Power Car	Stored, awaiting move to GCR(N)	East Midlands Trains
43089	HST Power Car	Stored, awaiting move to GCR(N)	East Midlands Trains
D4 *Great Gable*- (**44004**)	Class 44	Operational	BR Blue
45133	Class 45	Undergoing repair	BR Blue
D182 (**46045**)	Class 46	Operational	BR Blue
47401 *North Eastern*	Class 47	Operational	BR Blue
D1516 (**47417**)	Class 47	Undergoing restoration	BR Two Tone Green
47761	Class 47	Stored	Rail Express Systems

Number(s) (Operating Number Highlighted)	Type	Status	Livery
D1048 *Western Lady*	Class 52	Undergoing restoration	BR Blue
Ex-BR Electric Loco			
27000 *Electra*	Class 77 EM2	Static display	BR Black
Ex-Industrial Diesel Locos			
16038 *Andy*	Fowler 0-4-0DM	Undergoing restoration	Grey with Railfreight Coal Logo
D1114 *Albert Fields/ Emfour 9*	Hudswell Clarke 0-6-0	Undergoing overhaul	Green
416 *Needlesnoot*	Andrew Barclay 0-4-0	Undergoing overhaul	Blue
RS12 *George*	Motorail Simplex	Stored	Brown
RS9 *Zippy*	Motorail Simplex	Stored	Blue
441	Andrew Barclay 0-4-0	Undergoing repair	Blue
D1154 *Manton*	Hudswell Clarke 0-6-0	Undergoing restoration	Green
5337	Mercury Tractor 0-4-0	Stored	Blue
384139/D2959	Ruston and Hornsby 0-4-0DE	Undergoing overhaul	BR Green
Diesel Multiple Units			
51118	Class 100 DMBS	Undergoing restoration	Green
56097	Class 100 DTCL	Undergoing restoration	Green
51907	Class 108 DMBS	Operational	BR Blue/Grey
56490	Class 108 DTCL	Operational	BR Blue/Grey
50015	Class 114 DMBS	Stored	BR Blue
50019	Class 114 DMBS	Undergoing restoration	BR Green
56006	Class 114 DTCL	Undergoing restoration	BR Green
56015	Class 114 DTCL	Stored	BR Blue
51669	Class 115 DMBS	Stored	BR Green
59659	Class 115 TS	Stored	BR Green
51849	Class 115 DMBS	Stored	BR Green
51591	Class 127 DMBS	Operational	BR Green
59609	Class 127 TCL	Operational	BR Green
51625	Class 127 DMBS	Operational	BR Green
51610	Class 127 DMBS	Stored	BR Green
141113 (55513 + 55533)	Class 141 DMS + DMSL	Operational	WYPTE Metrotrain
142011 (55552 + 55602)	Class 142 DMS + DMSL	Operational	Northern Rail
142013 (55554 + 55604)	Class 142 DMS + DMSL	Operational	Northern Rail
Electric Multiple Units			
29666	Class 505 TS	Awaiting restoration	BR Blue
29670	Class 505 TS	Awaiting restoration	BR Blue
Ex-BR Steam Locos			
158A	MR 156 Class 2-4-0	Static	MR Maroon

Number(s) (Operating Number Highlighted)	Type	Status	Livery
47327	LMS Class 3F Jinty 0-6-0T	Static	S&DJR Prussian Blue
47357 (16440)	LMS Class 3F Jinty 0-6-0T	Undergoing overhaul	Primer
47445	LMS Class 3F Jinty 0-6-0T	Undergoing overhaul	Primer
47564	LMS Class 3F Jinty 0-6-0T	Stored	Primer
46203 *Princess Margaret Rose*	LMS Princess Royal Class 4-6-2	Stored	BR Maroon
6223 *Duchess of Sutherland*	LMS Coronation Class 4-6-2	Operational	LMS Crimson Lake
80079	BR Standard 4MT 2-6-4T	Undergoing overhaul	BR Lined Black
80080	BR Standard 4MT 2-6-4T	Operational	BR Lined Black
73129	BR Standard Class 5 4-6-0	Stored	BR Lined Black
92212	BR Standard 9F 2-10-0	Undergoing overhaul	BR Black
Ex-Industrial Steam Locos			
2111 *Lytham St. Annes*	Peckett 0-4-0ST	Operational	Lined Blue
1163 *Whitehead*	Peckett 0-4-0ST	Stored	BR Brunswick Green
1547 *Victory*	Peckett 0-4-0ST	Static	Dark Green
7214 *George*	RSH 0-4-0ST	Undergoing restoration	Dark Green
7817 *Castle Donington Power Station No 1*	RSH 0-4-0ST	Awaiting overhaul	Dark Blue
109 *Gladys*	Markham and Co. 0-4-0ST	Static	Dark Green
Stanton 24	Andrew Barclay 0-4-0TC	Static	Dark Green
Brown Bailey No 4	Nasmyth Wilson and Company 0-4-0ST	Plinthed	Light Blue
Boots No 2	Ruston and Hornsby 0-4-0DE	Static	Boots Blue

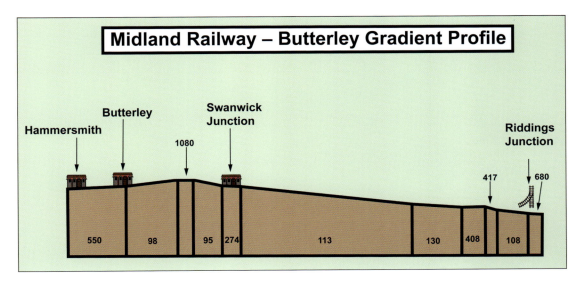

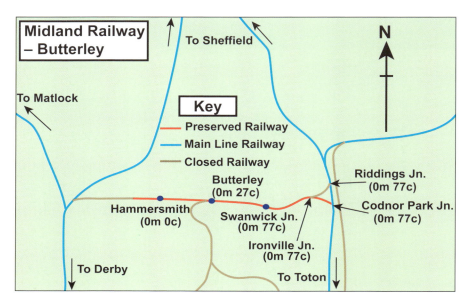

Class 45 45133 arrives at Swanwick Junction on 21 September 2013 on a service from Hammersmith to Ironville Junction.

Northampton & Lamport Railway

Built on part of the Northampton to Market Harborough branch line, the railway was opened in 1859 and closed in 1981. The preserved operation, based at Pitsford and Brampton station, has a 1⅖-mile long running line and was reopened in 1995.

Getting there: Bus services are indirect; at 5 miles from Northampton station, a taxi may be the best option. By car, parking at Pitsford station – NN6 8BD.

Refreshments: Platform 3 Buffet, hot drinks, snacks and hot food. Pub: Brampton Halt in former station buildings, 10 minutes' walk, Fuller's beers, hot food.

Future plans: On 14 November 2021, the first train (an engineer's special) ran to Broughton, with opening to the public due in 2022. A northern extension of around 3 miles to Spratton is planned.

Website: www.nlr.org.uk

Number(s) (Operating Number Highlighted)	Type	Status	Livery
Ex-BR Diesel Locos			
31289 *Phoenix*	Class 31	Operational	BR Experimental Blue
33053	Class 33	Operational	BR Blue
47205	Class 47	Operational	Railfreight Distribution
Ex-Industrial Diesel Locos			
21	Fowler 0-4-0	For scrap after spares	BR Green
53	Ruston and Hornsby 0-6-0	Undergoing repair	Black
764	Ruston and Hornsby 0-6-0	Operational	Green
Ex-Main Line Steam Locos			
3862	GWR 2884 Class 2-8-0	Undergoing restoration	Primer
5967	GWR 4900 Class 4-6-0	Undergoing restoration	Primer
Ex-Industrial Steam Locos			
776	Andrew Barclay 0-4-0ST	Undergoing restoration	Black
1378	Peckett 0-6-0ST	Undergoing restoration	Black
2104	Peckett 0-4-0ST	Awaiting overhaul	Blue
2323	Andrew Barclay 0-4-0ST	Undergoing restoration	BR Green

On 20 November 2005, 08359 powers a service on the Northampton & Lamport Railway, while 45118 awaits a return to service.

Nottingham Heritage Railway

Nottingham Heritage Railway (NHR), formerly known as Great Central Railway – Nottingham (GCR(N)), is based at Ruddington, south of Nottingham, and operates 10 miles south to Loughborough. Largely over Network Rail metals, the freight route serving the British Gypsum works at East Leake from the Midland Main Line. The NHR runs from Fifty Steps Bridge, where a branch leads to the main centre at Ruddington.

Getting there: Nottingham City Transport number 10 bus to 'The Green' in Ruddington village, then a ten to 15 minutes' walk. Free car parking at Ruddington – NG11 6JS.

Refreshments: Buffet at Ruddington, hot snacks and drinks. Pub: Frame Breakers, Ruddington, Nottingham beers and guests, hot food.

Future plans: Plans are in place for the construction of a high-level interchange station at Loughborough following the reinstatement of the connection with the Great Central Railway during the mid-2020s.

Website: www.gcrn.co.uk

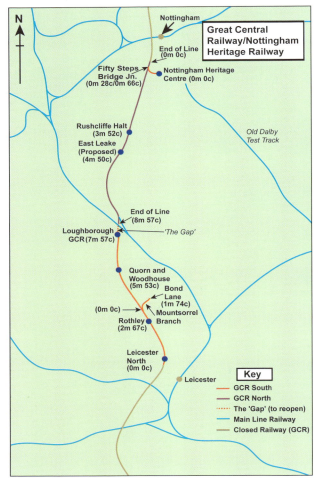

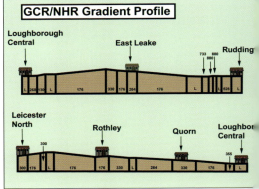

Number(s) (Operating Number Highlighted)	Type	Status	Livery
Ex-BR Diesel Locos			
03118 (D2118)	Class 03	Undergoing repair	BR Blue
08114 *Gotham*	Class 08	Operational	BR Blue
08220	Class 08	Operational	BR Blue
08694	Class 08	Awaiting restoration	EWS Maroon/Gold
D8154 (20154)	Class 20	Operational	BR Blue
D5830 (31563)	Class 31	Operational	BR Golden Ochre
37009	Class 37	Undergoing overhaul	BR Blue
43044	HST Power Car	Undergoing repair	InterCity Executive
43159	HST Power Car	Undergoing repair	First Group Blue
46010	Class 46	Undergoing restoration	BR Blue
47292	Class 47	Undergoing repair	BR Large Logo Blue
56097	Class 56	Operational	Railfreight Coal
Ex-Industrial Diesel Locos			
D2959 *Staythorpe*	Ruston and Hornsby 165 0-4-0DE	Awaiting repairs	BR Green
Diesel Multiple Units			
50645	Class 108 DMCL	Undergoing restoration	BR Blue/Grey
50926	Class 108 DMBS	Undergoing restoration	Primer
51138	Class 116 DMBS	Undergoing restoration	BR Green
51151	Class 116 DMS	Stored	BR Green
59501	Class 117 TCL	Stored	BR Green
144003 (55803 + 55826)	Class 144 DMS = DMSL	Operational	Northern Rail
Ex-Main Line Steam			
8274	LMS 8F 2-8-0	Stored	BR Black
70284	Alco S160 2-8-0	Undergoing overhaul	Black
Ex-Industrial Steam			
2015 *Arthur*	Manning Wardle 0-6-0ST	Stored	Primer
1762 *Dolobran*	Manning Wardle 0-6-0ST	Undergoing overhaul	Blue
2009 *Rhyl*	Manning Wardle 0-6-0ST	Undergoing overhaul	Green
1682 *Julia*	Hudswell Clarke 0-6-0ST	Undergoing overhaul	Primer

Left: **On 28 May 2016, the National Railway Museum's prototype HST 41001, backed by 47292, is seen at Fifty Steps Bridge Junction with a service for Loughborough from Ruddington on the GCR(N).**

Below: **Just south of Fifty Steps Bridge, D7629 (25279) from the East Lancashire Railway heads a train south towards Loughborough on 26 August 2007, with 47292 on the rear due to no run round being available at either end.**

Peak Rail

The former Midland Railway main line from Manchester Central to St Pancras was closed between Matlock and Buxton in 1968. After efforts to reopen the line failed in the 1970s, the preserved operation opened between Darley Dale and Matlock in 1991. The main depot and workshops are found at Rowsley.

Getting there: By foot, transfer from Matlock main line station to Matlock Riverside. Bus services from Derby, Nottingham and Chesterfield. By car, Rowsley South – DE4 2LF, Darley Dale – DE4 2EQ, Matlock – DE4 3NA.

Refreshments: Buffet with hot food at Rowsley South. Pub: Twenty Ten, Matlock, guest beers and hot food.

Future plans: The railway's intended next step is reopening the 4¼-mile extension to Bakewell. Longer term, heading west, the trackbed is used by the Monsal Trail but Peak Rail could share the pathway as a single line operation.

Website: www.peakrail.co.uk

Number(s) (Operating Number Highlighted)	Type	Status	Livery
Ex-BR Diesel Locos			
D2953	Class 01	Operational	BR Green
D2854	Class 02	Operational	BR Green
D2866	Class 02	Undergoing overhaul	Primer
D2139	Class 03	Operational	BR Green
D2199	Class 03	Undergoing overhaul	BR Green
03027	Class 03	Stored	BR Blue
03099	Class 03	Operational	BR Blue
03113	Class 03	Operational	BR Blue
03180	Class 03	Undergoing overhaul	BR Blue
D2205	Class 04	Operational	BR Green
D2229	Class 04	Operational	Black
D2272	Class 04	Stored	Blue
D2284	Class 04	Operational	BR Green
D2289	Class 04	Undergoing restoration	Red/Grey
D2337	Class 04	Stored	BR Green
D2587	Class 05	Stored	BR Green
D2420 (06003)	Class 06	Undergoing repair	BR Green
07001	Class 07	Operational	BR Blue
08016	Class 08	Operational	BR Blue
08830	Class 08	Undergoing overhaul	BR Blue
09001	Class 09	Operational	EWS Maroon/Gold
14901 (D9524)	Class 14	Undergoing repair (at Darley Dale)	BR Blue with Yellow Cab
D9525	Class 14	Undergoing overhaul	BR Two-Tone Green

Number(s) (Operating Number Highlighted)	Type	Status	Livery
D7659 (**25309**)	Class 25	Operational	BR Two-Tone Green
37310 *British Steel Ravenscraig* (37152)	Class 37	Operational	BR Large Logo Blue
D8 *Penyghent* (44008)	Class 44	Operational	BR Green
46035	Class 46	Stored	BR Blue
50029 *Renown*	Class 50	Stored	BR Large Logo Blue
50030 *Repulse*	Class 50	Undergoing overhaul	BR Large Logo Blue
97650	Class 97/6	Awaiting restoration	BR Blue
PWM654 (**97654**)	Class 97/6	Operational	BR Blue
Ex-Industrial Diesel Locos			
9120	EE 0-6-0	Operational	BR Green
146C	BR Class D2/12 0-6-0	Operational	BR Green
4220015	0-6-0	Operational	Black
4240015	0-6-0	Awaiting overhaul	Green
4200019	John Fowler 0-4-0DH	Green	Stored
27097	North British 0-4-0	Stored	Grey
319284	Ruston and Hornsby 0-4-0	Undergoing restoration	Blue
2 (423658)	Ruston and Hornsby 0-4-0	Undergoing restoration	Blue
284V	Thomas Hill 0-4-0	Operational	Blue
2654	Yorkshire Engine Co. 0-4-0	Stored	Blue
2679	Yorkshire Engine Co. 0-4-0	Stored	Yellow
2 (2675)	Yorkshire Engine Co. 0-4-0	Operational	
2480	Yorkshire Engine Co. 0-4-0DE	Stored	Yellow
319284	Ruston and Hornsby 0-4-0DM	Stored	Blue
BT803	Brush Traction 0-6-0	Stored	Blue
D1186	Hudswell Clarke 0-6-0DM	Operational	Blue
6295	Hunslet 0-6-0	Stored	Blue
27932	North British 0-6-0	Stored	Blue
10180	Sentinel 0-6-0	Stored	Blue
2940	Yorkshire Engine Co. 0-6-0	Undergoing overhaul	Grey
2679	Yorkshire Engine Co. 0-4-0DH	Stored	Yellow
Electric Multiple Units			
Hazel	Class 403 5-BEL TPFK	Awaiting restoration	Pullman
Car 87	Class 403 5-BEL TPT	Awaiting restoration	Pullman
4311 (61287 + 75407)	Class 414 2-HAP DMBSO + DTCL	Awaiting restoration	Network SouthEast

East Midlands

Number(s) (Operating Number Highlighted)	Type	Status	Livery
Ex-Mainline Steam Locos			
6634	GWR 0-6-2T		
5553	GWR 2-6-2T		
5224	GWR 2-8-0T		
Ex-Industrial Steam Locos			
3138	Hawthorn Leslie 0-6-0ST		
7063	Robert Stephenson and Hawthorns 0-4-0ST		
150 (3892)	Robert Stephenson and Hawthorns 0-6-0ST		
72	Vulcan Foundry		
65	Hudswell Clarke		

On 25 September 2008, the sole surviving example of the Class 06 fleet, 06003, gives brake van rides, top and tailed with Class 03 03099 at Rowsley.

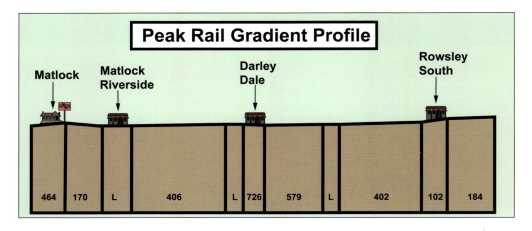

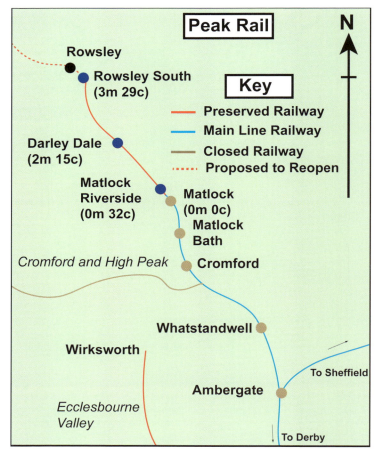

Chapter 5
West Midlands

Chasewater Railway

The Chasewater Railway, previously marketed as The Colliery Line, runs for 2 miles in a horseshoe configuration around the shores of Chasewater Lake in the eponymously named country park between Brownhills West and Chasetown in Staffordshire. The line was part of a network operated by the National Coal Board to serve the coalfields of the Cannock Chase area connecting with the Sutton Park line at Aldridge and with exchange sidings about ¼ mile north of Brownhills West station. Closure of Brownhills station due to the M6 Toll motorway led to the rebuilding of Brownhills West with a new carriage shed and heritage centre, and completion of the Chasetown section of the line (the 'Chasetown Extension Railway' between Chasewater Heaths and Chasetown Church Street).

Getting there: Bus services operate from Birmingham and Walsall (number 3 from Cannock, 10a from Walsall and 937 and 937a from Birmingham). Free parking is available at Brownhills West station, Pool Road – WS8 7NL.

Refreshments: The Sidings Tea Room, Brownhills West, provides hot food (including breakfast) and drinks. Pub: The Jiggers Whistle, Brownhills High Street, approximately 25 minutes' walk, wide beer selection but no food.

Future plans: A narrow gauge line is planned from Brownhills West to the entrance to the country park, but further expansion is currently unlikely.

Website: www.chasewaterrailway.co.uk

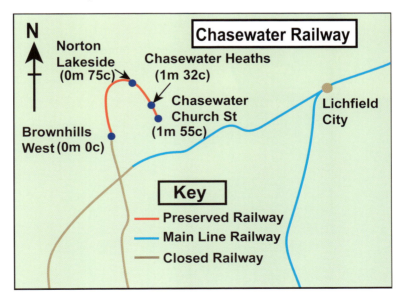

Number(s) (Operating Number Highlighted)	Type	Status	Livery
Ex-Industrial Diesel Locos			
No 4 (**3410**/1955)	Baguley 0-4-0	Awaiting repairs	Black
D2911 (27876)	North British 0-4-0DH	Operational	BR Green
27656	North British 0-4-0DH	Stored	Blue
8366	Bagnall/RSH 0-4-0DH	Operational	Black/yellow stripes
6678	Hunslet 0-4-0DH	Operational	NCB Blue
4220015 *Toad*	Fowler 0-4-0DH	Stored	Red
4100013	Fowler 0-4-0DM	Stored	Green
3097	Brush Bagnall 0-4-0DE	Undergoing overhaul	Green
20	Kent 4wDM Planet (Simplex)	On loan stored	Blue
1612	Kent 4wDM Planet (Simplex)	Operational	Blue
305306	Ruston 48DS 4wDM	Undergoing overhaul	Green
3119 *Hem Heath*	Bagnall 0-6-0DM	Stored	Blue
3208	Bagnall 4wDH	Stored	Blue
3027 Bass No 5	Baguley 0-4-0DM	Operational	Red
3590 Bass No 11	Baguley 0-4-0DM	Stored	Red
Derbyshire Stone No 2 – 1891	FC Hibberd Planet 4wDM No 20	Stored	Blue
1930 (15097)	Simplex 0-4-0PM	Operational	Black
2026 (15099)	Simplex 0-4-0PM	Operational	Black
Diesel Multiple Units			
59603	Class 127 TCL	Operational (as hauled stock)	Maroon
59444	Class 116 TC	Operational (as hauled stock)	Maroon
142027 (55568 + 55618)	Class 142 DMS + DMSL	Spares donor	Northern Rail
142029 (55570 + 55620)	Class 142 DMS + DMSL	Operational	Northern Rail
142030 (55571 + 55621)	Class 142 DMS + DMSL	Operational	Northern Rail
Ex-Industrial Steam Locos			
750	Hudswell Clarke 0-4-0T	Operational	Green
Holly Bank No 3 (3783)	Hunslet 0-6-0ST	Operational	Blue
S100 (**1822**)	Hudswell Clarke 0-6-0T	Overhaul	Red
Dunlop No 6 (**2648**)	Bagnall 0-4-0T	Operational	Blue
2937	Neilson and Co. 0-4-0T	Overhaul	Black
Kent No 2 (**2842**)	W G Bagnall 0-4-0ST	Awaiting overhaul	Red
2780	Hawthorne Leslie 0-4-0T	Awaiting overhaul	Green
2012	Peckett and Sons 0-4-0T	Awaiting overhaul	Green
No 5	Sentinel 0-4-0T	Awaiting overhaul	Brown
Sheepbridge No 15 (**431**)	Hudswell Clarke 0-6-0T	Stored	Green
917	Peckett and Sons 0-4-0T	Stored	Blue

Churnet Valley Railway

The Churnet Valley line was one of three original routes centred around Cheddleton, built by the North Staffordshire Railway, opening in 1849 from North Rode in Cheshire to Uttoxeter. The line was closed between 1964 and 1988, but part of the central section passed into the hands of a preservation society and today operates as the Churnet Valley Railway. The railway's main workshops and facilities are based at Cheddleton. The line between Leek and North Rode closed in June 1964 and, in January 1965, the passenger service was withdrawn over the section between Leek and Uttoxeter, and the line south of Oakamoor closed. Goods traffic was retained from Leek to Stoke and sand traffic to Oakamoor until 1988, enabling the preservation of the line to begin in earnest.

Getting there: Buses run from Hanley and Leek to Cheddleton with some buses from Stoke.

Refreshments: Signals Tea Rooms, Kingsley and Froghall Station, hot food and drinks. Pub: Black Lion, adjacent to Consall station, hot food and guest ales.

Future plans: Reopening through to Alton Towers and Stoke-on-Trent are long-sought aims; reopening to Leek with a new station to the south of the town is a shorter-term goal.

Website: www.churnetvalleyrailway.co.uk

Number(s) (Operating Number Highlighted)	Type	Status	Livery
Ex-BR Diesel Locos			
D3800 (08633)	Class 08	Operational	BR Green
D8057 (20057)	Class 20	Undergoing restoration	BR Green
25322 *Tamworth Castle*	Class 25	Awaiting restoration	BR Blue Yellow Cabs
33021	Class 33	Operational	Plain Red
33102 *Sophie*	Class 33	Awaiting repairs	BR Blue
Ex-Industrial Diesel Locos			
446	Andrew Barclay Sons and Co 0-4-0	Awaiting repairs	Green
610	Sentinel 0-8-0DH	Restoration	Blue
WD 70031	Andrew Barclay 0-4-0DM	Operational	Black
MOD 429	Ruston and Hornsby LSSH 0-6-0DH	Operational	Red
Ex-Main Line Steam			
5197	S160	Operational	Black
6046	S160	Operational	Black
48173	LMS 8F 2-8-0	Restoration	LMS Black
Ex-Industrial Steam			
2871	Fablok Polish TkH 49 0-6-0T	Stored	PKP Green
2944	Fablok Polish TkH 49 0-6-0T	Operational	PKP Green
2226	Andrew Barclay 0-4-0ST	Awaiting overhaul	Red

Britain's Preserved Railways

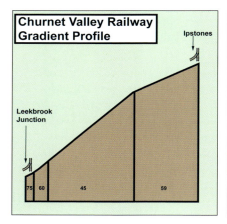

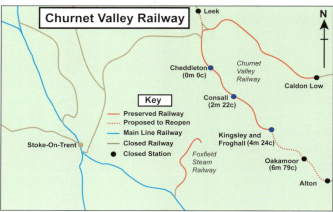

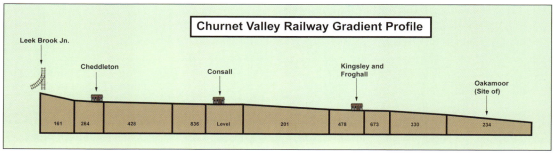

Visiting from the Severn Valley Railway, 20059 arrives at Cheddleton on 22 September 2012 with a train from Caldon Low.

Severn Valley Railway

Often regarded as Britain's premier heritage railway, the 16-mile-long Severn Valley Railway (SVR) is well funded and runs services through most of the year, with an extensive diesel gala usually held in May (featuring main line guests), and regular diesel-hauled services at other times (around 10 per cent of trains). The line, completed in 1862 by the West Midland Railway, was absorbed into the GWR the following year and linked Hartlebury and Shrewsbury via Stourport-on-Severn. The link from Bewdley to Kidderminster was opened in 1878. After closure in 1963, the northern section of the line was bought in 1965 by a group of local enthusiasts with the initial intention of running it from Bridgnorth to Alvely Colliery Sidings, near Highley. The line was purchased through to Foley Park in 1974 and finally extended through to Kidderminster in 1984. The major diesel workshops are sited at Kidderminster with some facilities, particularly for the 'Western' fleet, located at Bridgnorth. Steam is serviced mostly at Bridgnorth.

Getting there: Train to Kidderminster, and buses to Kidderminster, Bewdley and Bridgnorth. Some 297 services between Bridgnorth and Kidderminster call at Upper Arley. The 125 service from Stourbridge, Kidderminster and Bewdley to Bridgnorth calls at Highley with a 20-minute walk to Highley station. Paid parking at both Kidderminster – DY10 1QZ, and Bridgnorth – WV16 4AX.

Refreshments: Full meal service at buffets at Bridgnorth and Kidderminster. Pubs: King and Castle, Kidderminster station, drinks and hot food; Railwaymen's Arms, Bridgnorth station, drinks and bar snacks.

Future Plans: Plans for a major redevelopment at Bridgnorth station were approved by Shropshire Council in August 2016. Expansion in terms of track miles is problematical for the SVR, as it is confirmed that the trackbed north of Bridgnorth has been sold and there is no possibility of Severn Valley trains ever reaching Ironbridge and Shrewsbury, although the trackbed between both Coalport and Bridgnorth is still in place. The SVR owns the trackbed of the Bewdley to Hartlebury line to 300 yards south of Mount Pleasant Tunnel. In 2015, the railway announced that Rail Safety Solutions had taken a lease on the section to the tunnel from Bewdley to provide training for Network Rail apprentices as far as Mount Pleasant Tunnel, with rumours that this may be a precursor to reopening the section. Chiltern Railways has also approached the SVR with a view to extending some of its services through to Bewdley, with a possible Park and Ride station near Foley Park Halt, serving the safari park and a conference centre.

Website: https://www.svr.co.uk

Number(s) (Operating Number Highlighted)	Type	Status	Livery
Ex-BR Diesel Locos			
D3022 (08015)	Class 08	Operational	BR Green
D3586 (08471)	Class 08	Operational	BR Green
13201 (08133)	Class 08	Operational	BR Green
H3802 (08635)	Class 08	Conversion to hydrogen hybrid in progress	Primer
08896	Class 08	Spares donor	EWS Maroon/Gold
D4100 *Dick Hardy* (09012)	Class 09	Operational	BR Green
09107	Class 09	Operational	BR Blue
12099	Class 11	Undergoing overhaul	BR Black

Number(s) (Operating Number Highlighted)	Type	Status	Livery
D9551	Class 14	Operational	BR Golden Ochre
33108	Class 33	Undergoing repair	BR Blue
D7029	Class 35	Undergoing restoration	BR Blue
37308	Class 37	Awaiting restoration	Primer
D821 *Greyhound*	Class 42	Undergoing overhaul	BR Maroon
50007 *Hercules/Furious*	Class 50	Main Line Operation	GB Railfreight
50031 *Hood*	Class 50	Stored	InterCity Swallow
50033 *Glorious*	Class 50	Operational	BR Large Logo Blue
50035 *Ark Royal*	Class 50	Operational	BR Blue
50044 *Exeter*	Class 50	Main Line Operation	BR Blue
50049 *Defiance*	Class 50	Main Line Operation	GB Railfreight
D1013 *Western Ranger*	Class 52	Undergoing overhaul	BR Blue
D1015 *Western Champion*	Class 52	Undergoing repair	BR Blue
D1062 *Western Courier*	Class 52	Operational	BR Blue
Ex-Industrial Diesel Locos			
319290 (D2957)	Ruston 165DM 0-4-0	Operational	BR Green
D2960 *Silver Spoon*	Ruston and Hornsby 165DM 0-4-0	Operational	BR Green
D2961	Ruston 165DE 0-4-0	Operational	BR Green
Diesel Multiple Units			
50933	Class 108 DMBS	Active	BR Green
51941	Class 108 DMBS	Active	BR Green
52064	Class 108 DMCL	Active	BR Green
56208	Class 108 DTCL	Active	BR Green
59250	Class 108 TBSL	Active	BR Green
Ex-BR Steam Locos			
813	Port Talbot Railway 0-6-0ST	Operational	GWR Green
1501	GWR 1500 Class 0-6-0PT	Operational	BR Lined Black
4150	GWR 5101 Class 2-6-2T	Undergoing overhaul	Primer
4930 *Hagley Hall*	GWR 4900 Class Hall 4-6-0	Undergoing overhaul	GWR Green
7714	GWR 5700 Class 0-6-0PT	Operational	BR Unlined Black
2857	GWR 2800 Class 2-8-0	Operational	GWR Unlined Green
34027 *Taw Valley*	SR West Country 4-6-2	Operational	BR Lined Green
13268	LMS Stanier Mogul 2-6-0	Undergoing overhaul	LMS Black
43106	LMS Ivatt Class 4 4-6-0	Operational	BR Lined Black
75069	BR Standard Class 4 4-6-0	Operational	BR Lined Black
Ex-Industrial Steam Loco			
7170 *Welsh Guardsman*	Hunslet Austerity 0-6-0ST	Operational	Lined Navy Blue.
2047 *Warwickshire*	Manning Wardle 0-6-0ST	Undergoing overhaul	Green

West Midlands

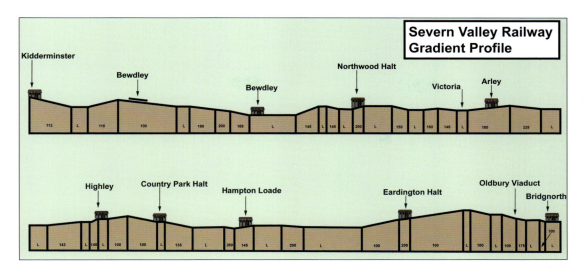

Below left: The Severn Valley Railway has the prestige and resources to attract a wide range of guest locomotives and, during the autumn steam gala in 2019, Southern Railway West Country 34092 *City of Wells* is seen at Foley Park with a Kidderminster to Bridgnorth service on 21 September. The loco is now based at the East Lancashire Railway.

Below right: In its first major visit away from its Didcot home after completion, new build GWR-design Saint 4-6-0 2999 *Lady of Legend* passes Foley Park on 24 April 2021.

Statfold Barn

The Statfold Barn Railway is a privately owned and operated mixed narrow-gauge railway near Tamworth. This was established by engineer Graham Lee (former chairman of the LH Group, buyers of Hunslet in 2005) around his farmhouse home and gardens. The project began with the purchase of the last steam loco built by Hunslet from the Trangkil sugar mill estate in Indonesia, a quest that led him to buy a number of other locos from the same railway for preservation. A 2ft gauge running line was also built around the site's lake, becoming the 'Garden Railway'.

Wabtec bought out LH Group in 2012 but Graham Lee kept the Hunslet rights. He had produced a completely new Hunslet steam loco in 2006. The site has expanded to include workshop facilities capable of extensive overhaul, restoration or even construction of new build locos, together with four stations. These are Statfold Junction (the main station next to the car park and entrance), Strawberry Park Halt, Oak Tree Halt and Cogan Halt. The latter is on the 'Balloon Loop' with no other road or foot access and is purely for lineside photographers. Access to the site is restricted to special event days and the operating lines are split into:

- The 'Upper' and 'Field Railways' 2ft (610mm) gauge lines running for approximately 1½ miles with a 'Balloon Loop' at one end; this was formerly a 2ft 6in (762mm) and 2ft (610mm) dual gauge line.
- A separate loop line 'Garden Railway' of 2ft (610mm) gauge runs around the ornamental lake.
- An 18in (457mm) mixed gauge tram track was laid in concrete parallel to the level section of the 'Field Railway'.

Getting there: There are no straightforward public transport links from Tamworth railway station to Statfold Barn, it being roughly a one hour walk of 3⅓ miles. The recommended taxi service is Smith's Taxis of Lichfield Street, Tamworth (01827 62777).

Refreshments: Diane's Diner, open only on event days and situated inside the Statfold Museum, with an outdoor seating area in the courtyard also provided. There are also mobile bars on event days, though with no real ale. Pub: Wolferstan Arms, Shuttington, beers and hot food.

Website: https://www.statfold.com

Builder	Wheel Arrangement	Works No	Name/Number	Build Date	Gauge	Status
Steam Locos						
Avonside	0-4-0T	1748	*Woolwich*	1916	18in	Restoration
Avonside	0-4-0T	2067	*Marchlyn*	1933	2ft	Operational
Bagnall	0-4-0ST	2091	*Wendy*	1919	2ft	Operational
Bagnall	4-4-T	2820	*Isibutu*	1945	2ft	Operational
Bagnall	0-4-2T	3023	*Isaac*	1953	2ft	Operational
Baldwin	4-6-0PT	44657	779	1916	2ft	Restoration
Barclay	0-4-0WT	1991	*Cegin*	1931	2ft	Operational
Beyer Peacock	0-4-4-0T	5292	K1	1909	2ft	Operational
Corpet	0-6-0PT	439	*Minas de Aller* No 2	1884	2ft	Operational
Davenport	0-4-0	1650	*Ryam Sugar* No 1	1917	2ft	Operational

Builder	Wheel Arrangement	Works No	Name/Number	Build Date	Gauge	Status
Etherington/Statfold	0-4-0CA	9902	*Sid*	2009	2ft	Operational
Fowler	0-4-2T	13355	*Saccharine*	1912	2ft	Operational
Hudswell Clarke	0-6-0ST	573	*Handy Man*	1900	3ft	Restoration
Hudswell Clarke	0-6-0	972	*Fiji CSR Lautoka No 11*	1912	2ft	Operational
Hudswell Clarke	0-4-0ST	1056	*CSR Lautoka No 19*	1914	2ft	Operational
Hudswell Clarke	0-6-0T	1172	*Alpha*	1922	2ft	Operational
Hudswell Clarke	0-6-0WT+T	1643	GP39 (*Bronllwyd*)	1930	2ft	Operational
Hunslet	0-4-0ST	299	*Hodbarrow*	1882	4ft 8½in	Static Display
Hunslet	0-4-0ST	492	*King of the Scarlets*	1889	1ft 10¾in	Static Display
Hunslet	0-4-0ST	542	*Cloister*	1891	2ft	Operational
Hunslet	0-4-0WT	684	*Jack*	1898	18 in	Operational
Hunslet	0-4-0ST	921	*Sybil Mary*	1906	2ft	Operational
Hunslet	0-4-0ST	995	*Gertrude*	1909	1ft 10¾in	Static Display
Hunslet	0-4-2T	1026	*Seaforth*	1910	2ft	Restoration
Hunslet	0-4-0ST	1709	*Michael*	1932	1ft 10¾in	Static Display
Hunslet	0-4-2T	1842	*Howard*	1936	2ft	Operational
Hunslet	0-4-2PT	3756	CDC No 1	1952	2ft	Restoration
Hunslet	0-4-2ST	3902	Trangkil No 4	1971	2ft	Operational
Hunslet	0-4-0ST	3903	*Statfold*	2005	2ft	Operational
Hunslet	0-4-0ST	3904	*Jack Lane*	2005	2ft	Operational
Jung	0-4-4-0T+T	4878	Jatibarang No 9	1930	2ft	Operational
Kerr Stuart	0-4-0ST	3128	*Roger* ISC No 2	1918	2ft	Operational
Krauss	0-4-2T	4045	Sragi No 1	1899	2ft	Operational
O&K	0-4-0WT+T	614	Pakis Baru No 1	1900	2ft 6in	Static Display
O&K	0-4-4-0T	1473	Pakis Baru No 5	1905	2ft 6in	Static Display
O&K	0-6-0WT+T	10750	*Max Sragi* No 14	1913	2ft	Operational
Peckett	0-6-0ST	1632	*Liassic*	1632	2ft	Operational
Peckett	0-6-0ST	2050	*Harrogate*	1944	2ft	Operational
Wilbrighton	0-4-0VB	2	*Howard*	2007	2ft	Operational
Petrol and Diesel Locos						
Baguley	0-4-0PM	680		1916	4ft 8½in	Stored
Brookville	4wDM	3526	*Charles*	1949	2ft	Operational
Brookville	4wDM	3746		1951	2ft	Operational
Funkey	4wDH	1001	D4	Unknown	2ft	Unrestored
Hudson	4wPM	36863		1929	2ft	Operational
Hudson	4wPM	39924	8	1931	2ft	Operational

Builder	Wheel Arrangement	Works No	Name/Number	Build Date	Gauge	Status
Hudswell	0-6-0DM	D1447	51 *Tom*	1981	2ft 6in	Static
Hunslet	0-4-0DM	2019		1939	2ft 6in	Operational
Hunslet	4wDM	2463	*Atlas*	1941	2ft	Operational
Hunslet	4wDM	2959		1944	2ft	Operational
Hunslet	0-4-4-0DM	4524	*Carnegie*	1954	2ft	Operational
Hunslet	4wDH	8819		1979	2ft	Operational
Hunslet	4wDH	9294		1991	2ft	Undergoing restoration
Hunslet	4wDM	9332		1994	2ft	Operational
Hunslet	4wDH	9351	*Murphy*	1994	2ft	Operational
Hunslet Taylor	4wDH	6720	W114H	1965	2ft	Operational
Hunslet Taylor	4wDH	7588	N13H	1968	2ft	Operational
Hunslet (Barclay Rebuild)	4wDH	7010		1971	2ft	Operational
Motor Rail	4wDM	435		1917	2ft	Undergoing repair
Motor Rail	4wPM	5226	*Brambridge Hall*	1930	2ft	Operational
Motor Rail	4wPM	4724	*Agwi Pet*	1939	2ft	Operational
Motor Rail	4w	8640		1941	2ft	Converted
Motor Rail	4wDM	9976	*Charley*	1954	2ft	Operational
Planet	4wDM	1776		1931	2ft	Operational
Plymouth	4wDM	1891		1924	2ft	Operational
Plymouth	4wDM	5800	*Tiny*	1954	2ft	Operational
Plymouth	4wDM	6137	*Tim*	1958	2ft	Operational
O&K	0-4-0DM	20777		1936	2ft	Operational
Road Machines	2wPH	8253		1959	Monorail	Static
Ruston & Hornsby	4wDM	201970	*Alistair*	1940	2ft	Operational
Vulcan	4wPM	4049	Inco No 3	1929	2ft	Operational
Electric Locos						
Bagnall (Greaves Rebuild)	0-4-0WE	1278	*The Coalition*	1890/1930	2ft	Restoration
Bagnall (Greaves Rebuild)	0-4-0WE	1445	*The Eclipse*	1895/1927	2ft	Restoration
Clayton	4wBE	5940a		1972	2ft	Operational
Greenwood and Batley	4wBE	420253		1970	2ft	Operational
Wingrove and Rogers	0-4-0BE	6092		1958	2ft 6in	Static

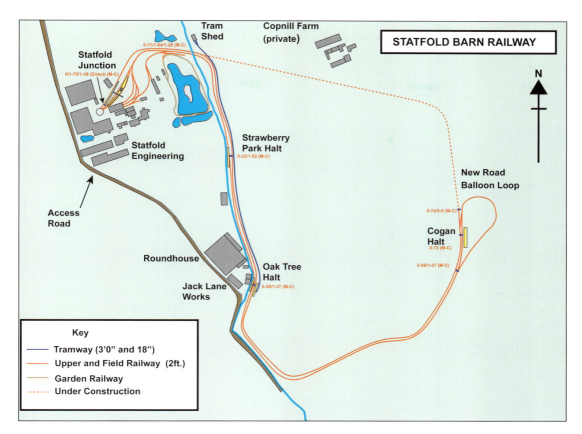

Above left: On 11 July 2021, 1953-built 2ft gauge Bagnall 0-4-2T *Isaac* approaches Strawberry Park Halt from Statfold Junction. The photo was taken from the top deck of the resident former Burton and Ashby Light Railway converted battery-powered tram.

Above right: At the lower end of gauge and loco size, 2ft gauge German O&K 0-4-0DM diesel 20777 unusually works a passenger service over the 'Garden Railway' at Statfold Barn on 11 September 2021, this substituting for an unavailable steam loco.

Chapter 6
Yorkshire

Embsay & Bolton Abbey Steam Railway

The Embsay & Bolton Abbey Steam Railway was opened in 1981, along part of the former Midland Railway route from Skipton to Ilkley. This originally opened in 1888 and was closed by British Rail in 1965, over 15 years before the reopening of part of the line. The route now runs for 4 miles from Embsay to Bolton Abbey station, which opened in 1997.

Getting there: Buses run from Skipton and Ilkley to Embsay station, the number 14 from Skipton (Monday–Friday) and Cravenlink Services 873 from Skipton, Ilkley and Bolton Abbey (Sundays/Bank Holidays). By car, free parking at Embsay station – BD23 6QX.

Refreshments: Bolton Abbey Station Tea Room/Embsay Coffee Shop, snacks and drinks. Pubs: Elm Tree Inn and Cavendish Arms, both five minutes' walk from Embsay station, food and beers.

Future plans: The medium-to-long-term aim is to run from Skipton through Embsay to Bolton Abbey, as there is track already in place, used by quarry trains for Swinden (Rylstone Quarry), and platforms are still in place at Skipton station. The project would require suitable rolling stock and reconnection of Embsay Junction. Shorter term could see a two-to-three-mile extension to Addingham, although redevelopment of the line on to Ilkley probably rules out full reopening.

Website: https://www.embsayboltonabbeyrailway.org.uk

Number(s) (Operating Number Highlighted)	Type	Status	Livery
Ex-BR Diesel Locos			
D2203	Class 04	Operational	BR Green
08054	Class 08	Stored	BR Blue
D3941 (08773)	Class 08	Operational	BR Green
D9513	Class 14	Operational	NCB Blue
31119	Class 31	Stored	BR Blue
D5600 (31435)	Class 31	Undergoing overhaul	BR Green
37294	Class 37	Operational	BR Blue
D1524 (47004)	Class 47	Stored	BR Two-Tone Green
Ex-Industrial Diesel Locos			
887	Ruston and Hornsby 4wDM	Operational	Green
4100003 *HW Robinson*	Fowler 0-4-0	Undergoing restoration	Green
4200003	Fowler 0-4-0	Stored	Brown
No 2 *Meaford*	Andrew Barclay 0-4-0	Operational	Green

Yorkshire

Number(s) (Operating Number Highlighted)	Type	Status	Livery
36	Hudswell Clarke 0-6-0	Undergoing restoration	Green
The Bug/Clockwork Orange	Baguley Drewry 4w	Stored	Green
Diesel Multiple Units			
142094 (55744 + 55790)	Class 142 DMS + DMSL	Operational	Northern Rail
3170	NER Petrol Electric Autocar	Operational	Non-standard NER Pink and Cream
3453	NER Autocoach	Undergoing restoration	Non-standard NER Pink and Cream
Ex BR Steam Locos			
52322	L&YR A Class/Class 27 0-6-0	Operational	BR Lined Black
Ex-Industrial Steam Locos			
68005 *Norman*	RSH Austerity 0-6-0ST	Operational	Black
2705 (No 7) *Beatrice*	Hunslet 0-6-0ST	Operational	Green
20 *Jennifer*	Hudswell Clarke 0-6-0ST	Operational	Green
1208 *Illingworth*	Hudswell Clarke 0-6-0ST	Operational	Green
140 *Thomas*	Hudswell Clarke PLA 0-6-0T	Awaiting overhaul	'Thomas' Blue
Slough Estates No 5	Hudswell Clarke 0-6-0ST	Undergoing overhaul	Green
1159 *Annie*	Peckett 0-4-0ST	Undergoing overhaul	Green
22 (2320)	Andrew Barclay 0-4-0ST	Undergoing overhaul	NCB Red
S121 (Primrose No 2)	Hunslet 0-6-0ST	Undergoing overhaul	NCB Red
8 *Warspite*	Hunslet 0-6-0ST	Awaiting overhaul	Primer
S112 *Revenge*	Hunslet 0-6-0ST	Awaiting overhaul	Blue
Monckton No 1	Hunslet Austerity 0-6-0ST	Awaiting overhaul	Blue
1440 *Airedale*	Hunslet 0-6-0ST	Awaiting overhaul	Brown
South Hetton No 69	Hunslet 0-6-0ST	Awaiting overhaul	Brown
S134 *Wheldale*	Hunslet	Awaiting overhaul	
York No 1	Yorkshire Engine Co.0-4-0ST	Stored	Green
BEA No 2	RSH 0-4-0T	Stored	Green

In National Coal Board colours, Hunslet 0-6-0T Austerity No 69 stands at Embsay with a train from Bolton Abbey on 27 December 2015.

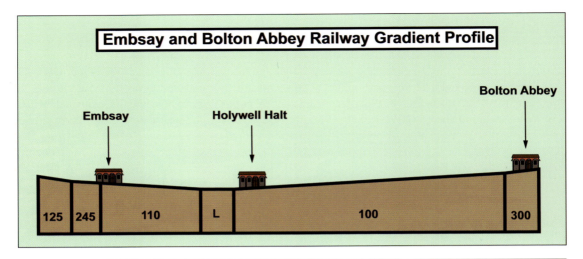

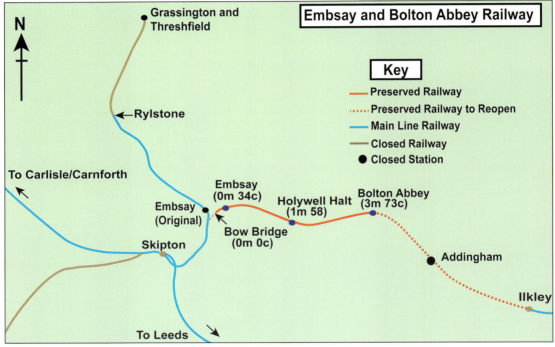

The BR Sectorisation era-liveried duo of 31119 and 37294 are seen at Embsay on 25 July 2009.

Keighley & Worth Valley Railway

The 4¾-mile branch line was opened in 1867, funded mostly by local mill owners with train operations 'franchised' to the Midland Railway, the operators of the Bradford/Leeds to Skipton line, which joined at the junction in Keighley. The Midland Railway bought out the Keighley and Worth Valley Railway (KWVR) Company and it became part of the London, Midland and Scottish Railway (LMS) at the 1923 Grouping. BR closed the branch in 1962, despite much local opposition, and the line was reopened by the KWVR Preservation Society (KWVRPS) in 1968. The sale of the branch was BR's first privatisation after a six-year legal battle to transfer ownership, with the company paying BR 25 yearly instalments up until 1992. The line features a number of well-preserved stations, including Damems, Haworth and Oakworth (famous from the film *The Railway Children*). The main depot and workshops are found at Haworth.

Getting there: Keighley has electrical multiple unit (EMU) services from Leeds and Bradford Forster Square every 30 minutes on Monday–Saturday, and hourly on Sundays. Keighley is also served by some longer-distance services from London, Lancaster, Morecambe and Carlisle. A through ticket is available from National Rail, giving a day rover for an £11 supplement. The number 500 bus from Todmorden and Hebden Bridge serves Oxenhope, Haworth and Keighley and is hourly Monday–Saturday, but has only three services on Sundays. Free car parking at Oxenhope – BD22 9LB.

Refreshments: Buffet with hot food and drinks at Keighley. Pub: certain trains feature a bar with cask ale. Listed in the Good Beer Guide under locations as 'Keighley to Oxenhope'.

Future Plans: Despite some speculation of an extension from Oxenhope to Hebden Bridge, this has never been a serious proposition. There is no other viable extension of the current branch. Commuter services may be introduced as an alternative to local buses, using diesel multiple units (DMUs).

Website: https://kwvr.co.uk

Number(s) (Operating Number Highlighted)	Type	Status	Livery
Ex-BR Diesel Locos			
D2511	BR Class D2/12 0-6-0	Operational	BR Green
08266	Class 08	Operational	Departmental Grey
08993 *Ashburnham*	Class 08	Operational	EWS Maroon/Gold
20031	Class 20	Operational	Railfreight Coal
25059	Class 25	Stored	BR Blue
37075	Class 37	Operational	Railfreight Triple Grey
D0226 *Vulcan*	English Electric 0-6-0	Operational	BR Green
Ex-Industrial Diesel Locos			
32 *Huskisson*	0-6-0DM	Operational	Black
431763 *James*	Ruston and Hornsby 0-4-0DE	Operational	Green
23 *Merlin*	Hudswell Clarke 0-6-0	Awaiting overhaul	Green
Diesel Multiple Units			
51189L	Class 101 DMBS	Operational	BR Green
51803	Class 101 DMCL	Operational	BR Green

Number(s) (Operating Number Highlighted)	Type	Status	Livery
50928	Class 108 DMBS	Awaiting overhaul	BR Green
51565	Class 108 DMCL	Awaiting overhaul	BR Green
79962	Waggon and Maschinenbau Railbus	Undergoing overhaul	BR Green
79964	Waggon and Maschinenbau Railbus	Operational	BR Green
143625 (55666 + 55691)	Class 143 DMS + DMSL	Spares donor	Arriva Trains Wales
144011 (55811 + 55834)	Class 144 DMS + DMSL	Operational	WYPTE Metrotrain

Ex-BR Steam Locos

Number(s) (Operating Number Highlighted)	Type	Status	Livery
51218 (68)	L&Y Pug 0-4-0ST	Stored	BR Black
1054	LNWR Coal Tank 0-6-2T	Undergoing overhaul	LNWR Unlined Black
85	Taff Vale Class O2 0-6-2T	Operational	TVR Lined Black
52044 (957)	L&Y Class 25 0-6-0	Operational	GNSR Lined Green
43924	MR 4F 0-6-0	Operational	BR Unlined Black
5775	GWR 5700 Class Pannier Tank 0-6-0PT	Stored	GN&SR Lined Ochre
47279	LMS Class 3F 0-6-0T	Stored	BR Black
41241	LMS Class 2MT 2-6-2T	Operational	KWVR Maroon
43924	MR 3835 Class 4F 0-6-0	Awaiting overhaul	BR Black
45212	LMS Class 5 Black 5 4-6-0	Operational	BR Lined Black
45596 *Bahamas*	LMS 5XP Jubilee Class 4-6-0	Operational	BR Lined Green
48431	LMS Class 8F 2-8-0	Awaiting overhaul	BR Black
78022	BR Standard Class 2MT 2-6-0	Operational	BR Lined Green
75078	BR Standard Class 4MT 4-6-0	Operational	BR Lined Black
80002	BR Standard 4MT 2-6-4T	Stored	BR Lined Black
5820	USA Class S160 2-8-0	Operational	USATC Grey
90733	WD Austerity 2-8-0	Undergoing overhaul	BR Black

Ex-Industrial Steam Locos

Number(s) (Operating Number Highlighted)	Type	Status	Livery
118 *Brussels*	Hudswell Clarke Austerity 0-6-0ST	Awaiting overhaul	LMR Blue
31 *Hamburg*	Hudswell Clarke 0-6-0T	Stored	Black
402 *Lord Mayor*	Hudswell Clarke 0-4-0ST	Stored	Green
1704 *Nunlow*	Hudswell Clarke 0-6-0T	Stored	Green
2258 *Tiny*	Andrew Barclay 0-4-0ST	Stored	Black
7069 *Southwick*	RSH 0-4-0 Crane Tank	Undergoing overhaul	Primer

Yorkshire

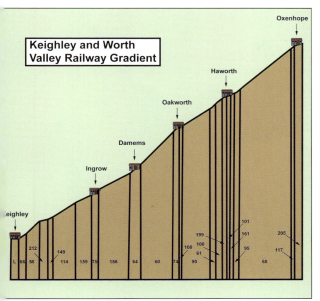

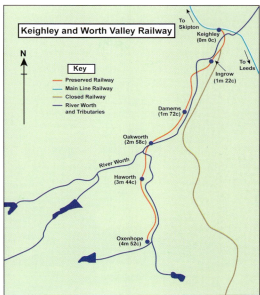

Lancashire and Yorkshire Class 25 0-6-0 957 passes the Top Field, made famous as a filming location from *The Railway Children*, with a rake of vintage carriages on 3 July 2011.

North Yorkshire Moors Railway

The Whitby and Pickering Railway was built as early as 1836 by George Stephenson, although Beeching marked the line for closure with passenger services ending in 1965 and freight the following year, before partial reopening in 1973. The 18-mile-long line runs from Pickering to Grosmont through the national park. The main workshop and depot are at Grosmont and the line features a testing gradient at 1 in 49 from there up to Goathland. Many services are extended over Network Rail metals to Whitby. The NYMR is thought to be the busiest steam heritage line in the world, with 355,000 passengers in 2010.

Getting there: Northern operates services through to Whitby, calling at Grosmont where a cross platform change is possible. Coastliner buses operate from Leeds and York through to Pickering, Goathland and Whitby, and also from Pickering to Scarborough. Car parks (not free) at Pickering – YO8 7AJ and Grosmont – YO22 5QE.

Refreshments: Buffet at Grosmont, breakfasts and some hot food; Pickering station buffet, breakfasts and some hot food. Pubs: The Station Inn, opposite Whitby station, guest beers, no food; Grosmont Crossing Club, Grosmont, opposite station, guest beers, no food and restricted opening times; The Sun Inn, Pickering, guest beers, no hot food.

Future plans: Reopening the 8-mile southern extension to Rillington Junction on the York–Scarborough line has long been discussed and is a policy objective for the North Yorkshire County Council. With substantial redevelopment of the trackbed in Pickering, this is very much a long-term aim.

Website: https://www.nymr.co.uk

The North Yorkshire Moors Railway makes full use of its permission to run through to Whitby over Network Rail metals, particularly in the summer months. Here Black 5 5428 *Eric Treacy* is leaving the popular Yorkshire fishing town on 16 September 2021, with a train for Pickering.

Number(s) (Operating Number Highlighted)	Type	Status	Livery
Ex-BR Diesel Locos			
D2207	Class 04	Undergoing overhaul	BR Green
08495	Class 08	Operational	BR Blue
08556	Class 08	Operational	BR Green
08850	Class 08	Operational	BR Blue
D5032 (24032)	Class 24	Undergoing overhaul	BR Green
D5061 (24061)	Class 24	Stored	BR Green
D7628 *Sybilla* (25278)	Class 25	Operational	BR Two-Tone Green
37264	Class 37	Operational	BR Large Logo Blue
Ex-Industrial Diesel Locos			
ED16	WD Drewry 0-4-0DM	Stored	NYMR Green
12139 *Redcar*	English Electric 0-6-0	Operational	BR Black
Diesel Multiple Units			
50160	Class 101 DMCL	Operational	BR Green
59539	Class 101 TCL	Operational	BR Green
50164	Class 101 DMBS	Operational	BR Green
50204	Class 101 DMBS	Stored	BR Green
51511	Class 101 DMCL	Stored	BR Green
Ex-BR Steam Locos			
926 *Repton*	SR V Class Schools 4-6-0	Operational	SR Olive Green
825	SR Class S15 4-6-0	Operational	SR Lined Olive Green
30830	SR Class S15 4-6-0	Stored	Primer
30841 *Greene King*	SR Class S15 4-6-0	Stored	Primer
34101 *Hartland*	SR West Country 4-6-2	Undergoing overhaul	Primer
1264	LNER B1 Class 4-6-0	Awaiting repairs	LNER Lined Black
63395	NER Class T2/Q6 0-8-0	Operational	BR Unlined Black
65894	NER Class P3 0-6-0	Operational	BR Unlined Black
5428 *Eric Treacy*	LMS 5MT Black 5 4-6-0	Operational	LMS Lined Black
44806	LMS 5MT Black 5 4-6-0	Undergoing overhaul	Primer
76079	BR Standard 4 2-6-0	Operational	BR Lined Black
75029 *The Green Knight*	BR Standard 4 4-6-0	Undergoing overhaul	BR Lined Green
80135	BR Standard 4 2-6-4T	Undergoing overhaul	BR Lined Green
80136	BR Standard 4 2-6-4T	Operational	BR Lined Black
92134	BR Standard 9F 2-10-0	Operational	BR Unlined Black
3672 *Dame Vera Lynn*	WD Austerity 2-10-0	Undergoing overhaul	Primer
Ex-Industrial Steam Locos			
Lambton Collieries No 29	Kitson and Co, 0-6-2T	Operational	LH&JC Apple Green
Lambton Collieries No 5	Kitson and Co, 0-6-2T	Stored	NCB Unlined Black
1625 *r*	Cockerill/Tramways de Bruxelles 0-4-0VBT	Operational	Dark Green

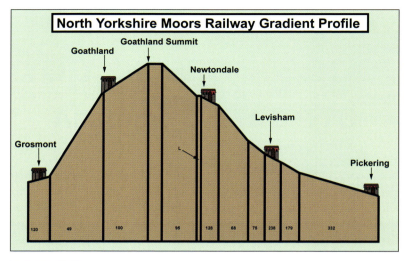
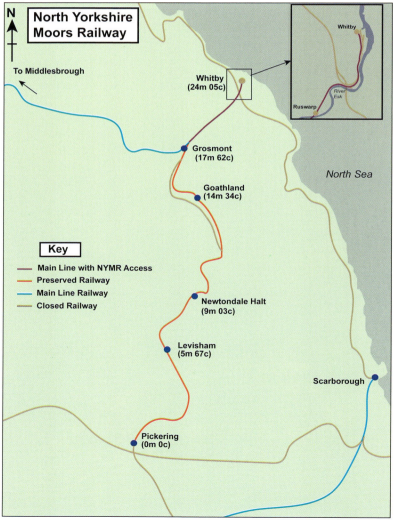

Wensleydale Railway

The Wensleydale Railway runs 22 miles from Northallerton West to Redmire. Opened between 1848 and 1878 as part of the East Coast to Settle and Carlisle route between Northallerton and Hawes Junction (now renamed as Garsdale), the line was closed to passengers in 1954. Most freight finished in 1992, and the line was latterly maintained by Network Rail for occasional military vehicle traffic from the nearby army bases. The main centre for operations of the preserved line is at Leeming Bar.

Getting there: Northallerton West is a 15-minute walk from Northallerton station, which is sited on the East Coast Main Line. Buses from Northallerton to Bedale, number 73 stops outside main line station. Free parking at Leeming Bar – DL7 9AR.

Refreshments: Platform One catering, Bedale, full food menu; Arthur's Tea Room, Leyburn, snacks and hot and cold drinks only. Pubs: Old Black Swan, Bedale, 10 minutes' walk, beers and food; Golden Lion, Leyburn, beers and food.

Future plans: The railway intends to consolidate running to Northallerton before extending westwards to Bolton Castle, Aysgarth and eventually Hawes. The extension through to Garsdale remains a long-term aim.

Website: https://wensleydale-railway.co.uk

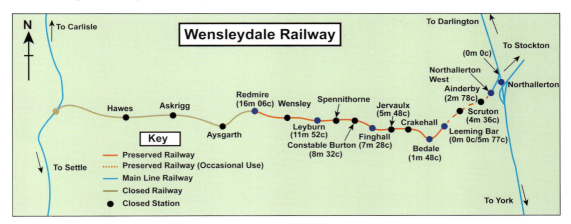

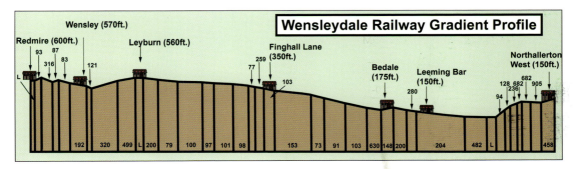

Number(s) (Operating Number Highlighted)	Type	Status	Livery
Ex-BR Diesel Locos			
03144	Class 03	Operational	BR Blue
D9523	Class 14	Operational	BR Maroon
20166	Class 20	Operational	HNRC Orange
33035	Class 33	Operational	BR Blue
37250	Class 37	Operational	Civil Engineer's 'Dutch'
47785	Class 47	Awaiting overhaul	EWS Maroon/Gold
Diesel Multiple Units			
51210	Class 101 DMBS	Undergoing restoration	BR Green
53746	Class 101 DMCL	Awaiting restoration	BR Blue/Grey
50256	Class 101 DMBS	Stored	BR Blue
56343	Class 101 DTCL	Stored	BR Blue
51572	Class 108 DMCL	Stored	BR Green
56274	Class 108 DTCL	Stored	Non-standard Carmine and White
51353	Class 117 DMBS	Static community room	Light Blue
51400	Class 117 DMS	Stored	BR Blue
59500	Class 117 TCL	Stored	Non-standard Carmine and BR Green
59509	Class 117 TCL	Stored	BR Blue/Grey
55032	Class 121 DMBS	Operational	BR Green
RDB975874	LEV 1 Railbus	Awaiting restoration	Yellow
142018 (55559 + 55609)	Class 142 DMS + DMSL	Stored	Northern Rail
142028 (55569 + 55619)	Class 142 DMS + DMSL	Operational	Northern Rail
142035 (55576 + 55626)	Class 142 DMS + DMSL	Spares donor	Northern Rail
142041 (55582 + 55632)	Class 142 DMS + DMSL	Undergoing restoration	Northern Rail
142060 (55710 + 55756)	Class 142 DMS + DMSL	Operational	Northern Rail
142078 (55728 + 55774)	Class 142 DMS + DMSL	Stored	Northern Rail
142087 (55737 + 55783)	Class 142 DMS + DMSL	Stored	Northern Rail
142090 (55740 + 55786)	Class 142 DMS + DMSL	Stored	Northern Rail
143623 (55664 + 55689)	Class 143 DMS + DMSL	Stored	Arriva Trains Wales
144020 (55820 + 55856 + 55842)	Class 144 DMS + MS + DMSL	Awaiting repairs	Northern Rail
Ex-BR Steam Locos			
69023 *Joem*	Class J72 0-6-0T	Awaiting overhaul	BR Apple Green

National Railway Museum-owned Deltic 55002 *The King's Own Yorkshire Light Infantry* arrives at Leyburn on 24 September 2011, with a service from Leeming Bar.

Chapter 7
North West

East Lancashire Railway

The East Lancashire Railway (ELR) runs for 12½ miles between Heywood and Rawtenstall and is formed from the remnants of two historical lines that served Bury. One to Bacup via Rawtenstall opened in 1846 as part of the original East Lancashire Railway, and the other to Rochdale and Manchester Victoria via Heywood, opened by the Lancashire and Yorkshire Railway in 1848. BR withdrew passenger services between Bury and Heywood in 1970 and Bury and Rawtenstall in 1972. It reopened from Bury to Ramsbottom as the ELR in 1987.

Getting there: Tram from Manchester Piccadilly or Manchester Victoria. There is also a bus service from Bury to Bolton for passengers to and from the northwest. Free car parking in Ramsbottom. Car Park (not free) at Bury Station – BL9 0EY.

Refreshments: Trackside Bar on platform at Bury, 12 guest beers and hot food; Buffer Stops at Rawtenstall station, ten guest beers, no hot food.

Future plans: An extension from Rawtenstall to Bacup is impractical after building development over the trackbed. The railway plans to extend eastwards from Heywood to a new station at Castleton Village, with a later possible interchange with Calder Valley main line trains, though plans for a new extension to the Manchester Metro system may affect the preserved operation.

Website: https://www.eastlancsrailway.org.uk

Number(s) (Operating Number Highlighted)	Type	Status	Livery
Ex-BR Diesel Locos			
D2956	Class 01	Operational	BR Black
D2062 (03062)	Class 03	Operational	BR Green
07013	Class 07	Stored	BR Blue
08164 *Prudence*	Class 08	Operational	BR Blue
13594 (08479)	Class 08	Awaiting repairs	BR Black
08944	Class 08	Awaiting repairs	BR Black
09024	Class 09	Operational	Departmental Grey
D9502	Class 14	Undergoing restoration	BR Two-Tone Green
D9531 *Ernest*	Class 14	Operational	BR Two-Tone Green
D8233	Class 15	Undergoing restoration	BR Green
D5054 *Phil Southern* (24054)	Class 24	Operational	BR Green
25279	Class 25	Operational	BR Blue
D5705	Class 28	Undergoing restoration	BR Green

Number(s) (Operating Number Highlighted)	Type	Status	Livery
33046	Class 33	Spares donor	South West Trains Blue
33109 *Captain Bill Smith RNR*	Class 33	Operational	Departmental Grey
6536 (33117)	Class 33	Undergoing overhaul	BR Blue
D7076	Class 35	Operational	BR Blue
37109	Class 37	Operational	BR Blue
37418 *An Comunn Gaidhealach*	Class 37	Main line operation	BR Large Logo Blue
40106 *Atlantic Conveyor*	Class 40	Operational (on loan to SVR)	BR Green
40135	Class 40	Awaiting repairs	BR Blue
40145	Class 40	Operational (on loan to Locomotive Services)	BR Green
D832 *Onslaught*	Class 42	Operational	BR Blue
45108	Class 45	Operational	BR Blue
45135	Class 45	Undergoing overhaul	BR Blue
D1501 (47402)	Class 47	Operational	BR Two-Tone Green
47765	Class 47	Operational	ScotRail
50015 *Valiant*	Class 50	Operational	BR Large Logo Blue
D1041	Class 52	Undergoing restoration	BR Blue
56006	Class 56	Operational	BR Blue
Ex-Industrial Diesel Locos			
9009	Motorail Simplex 4WDM	Operational	Green
4002 *Billy*	MSC Hudswell Clarke	Operational	Black
3438	FC Hibberd Planet	Undergoing restoration	Blue
Diesel Multiple Units			
50455	Class 104 DMBS	Operational	BR Blue
50517	Class 104 DMCL	Operational	BR Blue
50437	Class 104 DMBS	Stored	Network SouthEast
50494	Class 104 DMSL	Stored	BR Blue
59137	Class 104 TCL	Stored	BR Green
59228	Class 104 TBSL	Stored	BR Blue
51485	Class 105 DMBS	Operational	BR Green
56121	Class 105 DTCL	Operational	BR Green
51813	Class 110 DMBC	Operational	BR Green
51842	Class 110 DMCL	Operational	BR Green
59701	Class 110 TSL	Operational	BR Green
56289	Class 121 DTS	Undergoing overhaul	BR Blue
55001	Class 122 DMBS	Operational	BR Blue
Diesel Electric Multiple Units			
8099	NIR Class 80	Spares/storage vehicle	NIR

Number(s) (Operating Number Highlighted)	Type	Status	Livery
Electric Multiple Units			
70549	Class 411 TSOL	Stores coach	BR Green
65451	Class 504 DMBSO	Under restoration as hauled stock	GMPTE Orange/Brown
77172	Class 504 DTSO	Under restoration as hauled stock	GMPTE Orange/Brown
Ex-BR Steam Locos			
52322	L&YR A Class 0-6-0	Operational	BR Black
752	L&YR 23 Class 0-6-0ST	Operational	Black
13065 (42765)	LMS Crab 2-6-0	Undergoing overhaul	LMS Maroon
60009 *Union of South Africa*	LNER A4 Class 4-6-2	Stored	BR Blue
34092 *City of Wells*	SR West Country 4-6-2	Operational	BR Lined Green
80080	BR Standard 4 2-6-4T	Operational	BR Lined Black
80097	BR Standard 4 2-6-4T	Operational	BR Lined Black
3855	GWR 2800 Class 2-8-0	Undergoing overhaul	Primer
7229	GWR 7200 Class 2-8-2T	Awaiting overhaul	Primer
Ex-Industrial Steam Locos			
32 *Gothenburg*	MSC Hudswell Clarke 0-6-0T	Operational	Thomas Blue
7232 *Ann*	Sentinel 0-4-0VBGT	Operational	Bronze Green
1	Andrew Barclay 0-4-0ST	Static	Blue

Warship D832 *Onslaught* approaches Ramsbottom on a train from Rawtenstall to Heywood on 5 July 2019.

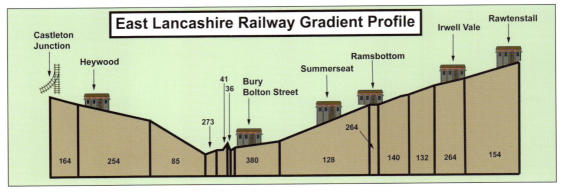

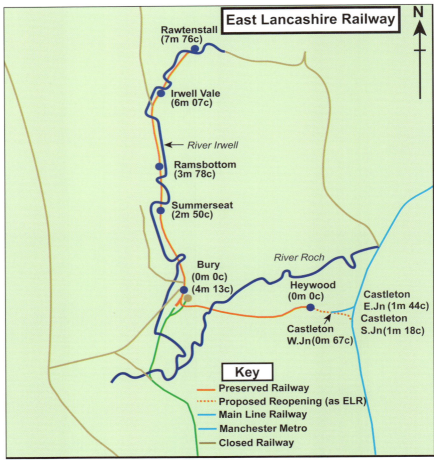

Lakeside & Haverthwaite Railway

This original Furness Railway branch line opened in 1869, running from Ulverston to Lakeside, with the 3½-mile-long section from Haverthwaite to the terminus preserved today. Connections are made with steamers on the 10-mile-long Lake Windermere. Haverthwaite is the main base and workshops.

Getting there: Buses to Haverthwaite (6/X6 from Ulverston Library), boats to Lakeside. Free car parking at Haverthwaite – LA12 8AL.

Refreshments: Full buffet with hot food at Haverthwaite. Pub: Anglers Arms, Haverthwaite, five minutes' walk, Thwaites beers, hot food.

Future plans: Despite rumours of a southward extension to Greenodd Road, redevelopment would appear to have ruled this out.

Website: https://www.lakesiderailway.co.uk

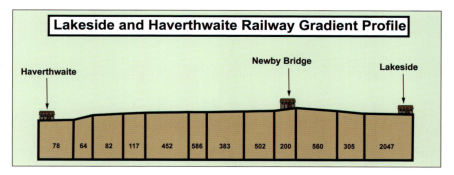

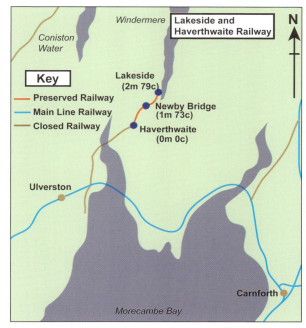

Number(s) (Operating Number Highlighted)	Type	Status	Livery
Ex-BR Diesel Locos			
D2072 (**03072**)	Class 03	Operational	BR Black
D2117	Class 03	Operational	Red
7120 (AD601/WD70272))	Class 11	Operational	Black
20214	Class 20	Operational	BR Green
Ex-Industrial Diesel Locos			
2098 *Rachel*	Motor Rail and Tram Car Co. 0-4-0	Undergoing restoration	Green
Diesel Multiple Units			
52071	Class 110 DMBC	Operational	BR Green
52077	Class 110 DMCL	Operational	BR Green
Ex-BR Steam Locos			
42073	LMS Fairburn 4MT 2-6-4T	Operational	BR Lined Black
42085	LMS Fairburn 4MT 2-6-4T	Undergoing overhaul	BR Lined Black
Ex-Industrial Steam Locos			
1245	Barclay 0-6-0ST	Operational	NCB Dark Blue
2333 *David*	Barclay 0-4-0ST	Operational	Maroon
2682 *Princess*	Bagnall 0-6-0ST	Operational	Dark Blue
3698 *Repulse*	Hunslet 0-6-0ST	Operational	Lined Black
2996 *Victor*	Bagnall 0-6-0ST	Operational	Maroon

On 9 June 2007, the two surviving LMS 2-6-4T Fairburn tanks, 42073 and 42085, arrive at Haverthwaite on a train from Lakeside.

Chapter 8

North East

Weardale Railway

Opened in 1842 by the Bishop Auckland and Weardale Railway, as part of the through branch from Bishop Auckland to Weardale, the line was used for the transport of limestone for the iron industry. The line was closed to passengers from 1953, staying open for freight to Eastgate until 1992. The railway reopened from Bishop Auckland to Stanhope in 2010 and is now owned by the Auckland Project, a County Durham-based charity. The headquarters of the line are at Stanhope and, at 18 miles long, it is one of the longest privately operated lines in the UK. Much of the traffic on the line revolved around the seasonal and lucrative Polar Express trains, with summer services also operated between Stanhope and Bishop Auckland.

Getting there: Bishop Auckland offers a main line connection with services from Darlington. Car parking at Wolsingham – DL13 3BL.

Refreshments: No 40 café at Stanhope station, hot drinks and snacks. Pub: The Grey Bull, Stanhope, guest beers, no food; Black Lion, Wolsingham, a National Cider Awards pub.

Future plans: Beyond Eastgate, some of the trackbed has been built on, although the line to this point is substantially intact. A lack of resources means further extension of running is unlikely in the near future.

Website: https://www.weardale-railway.org.uk

Number(s) (Operating Number Highlighted)	Type	Status	Livery
Ex-BR Diesel Locos			
31285	Class 31	Operational	Network Rail Yellow
31459	Class 31	Undergoing overhaul	BR Blue with Grey Roof
31465	Class 31	Stored	Network Rail Yellow
Diesel Multiple Units			
50980	Class 108 DMBS	Operational	BR Green
52054	Class 108 DMCL	Operational	BR Green
55012	Class 122 DMBS	Operational	BR Green
144010 (55810 + 55833)	Class 144 DMS + DMSL	Operational	Northern Rail
Ex-Industrial Steam Locos			
40	RSH 0-6-0T	Overhaul	Black

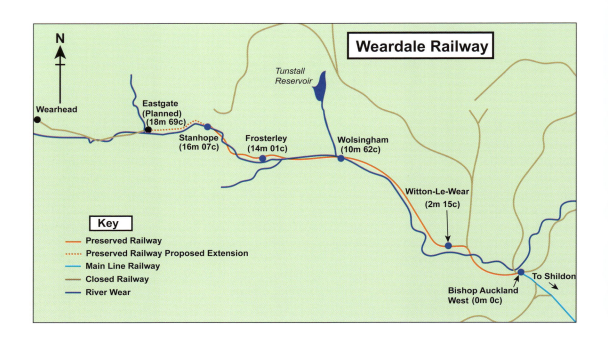

Chapter 9
Scotland

Bo'ness & Kinneil Railway

The Bo'ness Railway is operated by the Scottish Railway Preservation Society (SRPS) over 5 miles of track between Bo'ness and Manuel Junction, which is adjacent to the Glasgow to Edinburgh main line via Falkirk. The line was opened in 1851, as part of the Slammanan and Borrowstounness Railway, before being absorbed into North British Railway in 1865. The preserved line began in 1979 with buildings and equipment imported from other areas of Scotland. The line was extended to Kinneil in 1987; this section was built from scratch, not being part of the original branch, and the original station is now the site of a roundabout on the road that runs parallel to the line. The railway was extended to Birkhill in 1989, and finally to Manuel in 2010, enabling main line access for SRPS stock transfers for railtours. The main depot and workshops are sited at Bo'ness.

Getting there: The nearest main line station is Linlithgow. Regular bus services run to Bo'ness from the bus stop outside the Four Marys (pub), which is opposite the Linlithgow Cross. Bo'ness station has free parking – EH51 9AQ.

Refreshments: Bo'ness station buffet, snack and drinks only. Pub: The Corbie Inn, Brewpub, 15 minutes' walk from Bo'ness station, three beers on tap and full food menu, highly recommended.

Future plans: A new station is planned for Manuel and a proposed extension from Bo'ness Low Junction (near Manuel) to an interchange with the Union Canal, near the former Causeway End Junction, is being investigated.

Website: https://www.bkrailway.co.uk

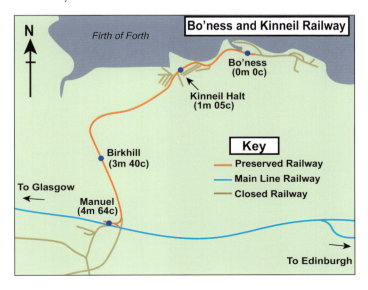

Number(s) (Operating Number Highlighted)	Type	Status	Livery
Ex-BR Diesel Locos			
D2767	North British Class D2/10	Operational	BR Green
D3558 (08443)	Class 08	Operational	BR Green
20020	Class 20	Operational	BR Blue
25235	Class 25	Undergoing overhaul	BR Blue
26024	Class 26	Operational	BR Blue
26038 *Tom Clift 1954-2012*	Class 26	Undergoing overhaul	BR Blue
27001	Class 27	Operational	BR Blue
27005	Class 27	Static exhibit	BR Blue
37025 *Inverness TMD*	Class 37	Main line operation	BR Large Logo Blue
37067 (37703)	Class 37	Operational	DRS Blue
37214	Class 37	Spares donor	West Coast Maroon
37261	Class 37	Awaiting restoration	DRS Blue
37403	Class 37	Main line operation	BR Large Logo Blue
47643	Class 47	Operational	InterCity ScotRail
Ex-BR Electric Locos			
84001	Class 84	Static display	BR Blue
Ex-Industrial Diesel Locos			
No 7	Ruston & Hornsby 4w Diesel-Mechanical 88DS 0-4-0	Stored	Green
P6687	Ruston and Hornsby 4w 0-4-0	Operational	Green
262998	Ruston & Hornsby 4w Diesel-Mechanical 88DS 0-4-0	Static display	Green
321733	Ruston & Hornsby 4w Diesel-Mechanical 88DS 0-4-0	Operational	Green
Clyde Iron Works No 1	NBL 4w 0-4-0DE	Static display	Green
Clyde Iron Works No 3	NBL 4w 0-4-0DE	Static display	Green
802	Ruston and Hornsby 4w 0-4-0DH	Stored	Primer
110U082	Motor-Rail Simplex 3ft gauge 4w 0-4-0DM	Stored	Green
Diesel Multiple Units			
51017	Class 126 DMSL	Operational	BR Green
59404	Class 126 TCL	Operational	BR Green
79443	Class 126 TRBF	Body restoration	BR Green
51043	Class 126 DMBS	Operational	BR Green
Electric Multiple Units			
75597 (303032)	Class 303 DTSO	Awaiting restoration	Strathclyde Black and Orange
61503 (303023)	Class 303 MBSO	Awaiting restoration	SPT Carmine and Cream

Scotland

Number(s) (Operating Number Highlighted)	Type	Status	Livery
75602 (303032)	Class 303 BDTSO	Awaiting restoration	Strathclyde Black and Orange
Ex-BR Steam Locos			
246	LNER D49 4-4-0	Undergoing overhaul	LNER Green
49	Caledonian Railway 449 Class 0-4-4T	Operational	Caledonian Blue
80105	BR Standard 4 2-6-4T	Undergoing overhaul	BR Black
45170	LMS Class 8F 2-8-0	Restoration	BR Black
Ex-Industrial Steam Locos			
NCB No 1	Neilson Reid 0-6-0ST	Operational	'Thomas' Blue
No 3	Andrew Barclay 0-4-0T	Stored	Dark Green
No 5	Hunslet Austerity 0-6-0ST	Awaiting restoration	Primer
68007 (NCB No 7)	Hunslet Austerity 0-6-0ST	Major repairs	BR Black
NCB No 19	Hunslet Austerity 0-6-0ST	Operational	NCB Green
No 17	Hunslet Austerity 0-6-0ST	Awaiting restoration	Primer
WPR No 20	Andrew Barclay 0-6-0T	Undergoing restoration	WPR Brown
No 24	Andrew Barclay 0-6-0T	Stored	NCB Black
3640	Hawthorn Leslie 0-4-0ST	Stored	'Percy' Green
4	Andrew Barclay 0-4-0ST	Awaiting restoration	NCB Black

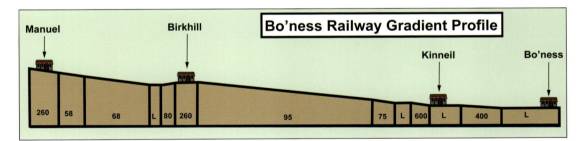

27001, accompanied by 26024, stands at Bo'ness on 29 December 2012 with a service for Manuel, with 47643 proving electric train heating at the rear.

Strathspey Railway

The line, running 10 miles from Aviemore to Broomhill via Boat of Garten, was part of the former Inverness and Perth Junction Railway from Aviemore to Forres. Passenger services were withdrawn in 1965 and resumed in preservation in 1978. The main shed and workshops are based in Aviemore.

Getting there: A main line cross platform connection has been built at Aviemore. Free parking at Aviemore – PH24 3BH.

Refreshments: Snacks and drinks only at Aviemore station buffet. Pub: Cairngorm Hotel, Aviemore, opposite the main line station, Cairngorm Beers and hot food.

Future plans: The railway intends to extend to Grantown-on-Spey with the aid of government money to divert the current A95 road from the original trackbed. Costs have now risen, and the project is currently on hold and viewed as a long-term aim.

Website: https://www.strathspeyrailway.co.uk

Number(s) (Operating Number Highlighted)	Type	Status	Livery
Ex-BR Diesel Locos			
D2774	Class D2/10	Operational	BR Green
D3805 (08490)	Class 08	Operational	BR Green
D5302 (26002)	Class 26	Stored	BR Green
D5325 (26025)	Class 26	Undergoing overhaul	BR Blue
D5394 (27050)	Class 27	Operational	BR Green
D5862 (31327)	Class 31	Operational	BR Green
37674	Class 37	Operational	Railfreight Red Stripe
Ex-Industrial Diesel Locos			
517 *Power of Enterprise*	Andrew Barclay and Son 0-4-0DH	Stored	BR Green
27549 (200518)	North British 0-4-0DM	Stored	Green
265618	Ruston and Hornsby 0-4-0DM	Operational	
260756	Andrew Barclay and Son 0-4-0DH	Stored	BR Green
Diesel Multiple Units			
51990	Class 107 DMBS	Stored	Strathclyde Black and Orange
52008	Class 107 DMBS	Stored	BR Green
52030	Class 107 DMCL	Awaiting restoration	BR Green
56047	Class 114 DTCL	Awaiting restoration	BR Green
51367	Class 117 DMBS	Operational	BR Green
51402	Class 117 DMS	Operational	BR Green
59511	Class 117 TCL	Undergoing restoration	BR Green
Ex-BR Steam Locos			
828	CR 812 Class 0-6-0	Operational	Caledonian Blue

Scotland

Number(s) (Operating Number Highlighted)	Type	Status	Livery
46512 *E.V. Cooper Engineer*	LMS Ivatt 2MT 2-6-0	Operational	Lined BR Black
46464	LMS Ivatt 2MT 2-6-0	Undergoing repair	Lined BR Black
5025 (45025)	LMS Black 5 4-6-0	Operational	BR Lined Black
Ex-Industrial Steam Locos			
2 (2020)	Andrew Barclay & Son 0-4-0ST	Stored	Green
9	RSH WD Austerity 0-6-0ST	Overhaul	Primer/NCB Black
48 (17)	Andrew Barclay & Son 0-6-0T	Awaiting overhaul	Blue

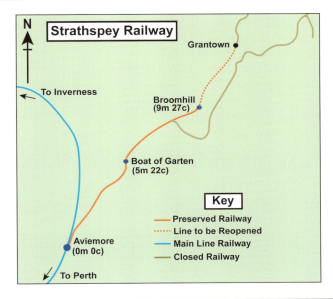

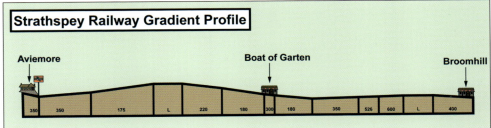

On 28 December 2014, Ivatt 2MT 2-6-0 46512 *E.V. Cooper Engineer* stands at Aviemore with a train for Boat of Garten. In the background, the daily Inverness to King's Cross 'Highland Chieftain' HST service departs.

Chapter 10
Wales

Llangollen Railway

Built on the former Ruabon to Barmouth line, the railway runs 10 miles from Llangollen to Corwen through the Dee Valley. Opened in 1865 and absorbed by the GWR in 1896, the line was closed to passengers by BR in 1965. The line was reopened in 1975 at Llangollen and gradually extended westwards. In 2011, work started on the 2½ mile section of track past the site of the closed Bonwm Halt to Corwen. The project was completed in 2014, with special trains running on 22 October to the new station at Corwen East for those who had contributed to the project. Regular passenger services to Corwen East started on 27 October 2014. The official opening took place on 1 March 2015.

Getting there: Bus service number 5 from Ruabon. On street parking near Llangollen station – LL20 8SN.

Refreshments: A full buffet at Llangollen serves hot food and drinks. Pub: Three Eagles Bar & Grill, 5 minutes' walk, Big Hand/Purple Moose beers and one guest beer, hot food.

Future plans: The next stage of the expansion of the railway westwards would be initially 3 miles to Trevor, with a longer-term aim of running on towards Bala.

Website: https://llangollen-railway.co.uk

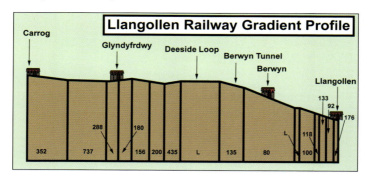

Wales

Number(s) (Operating Number Highlighted)	Type	Status	Livery
Ex-BR Diesel Locos			
03162	Class 03	Awaiting repairs	BR Blue
13265 (**08195**)	Class 08	Operational	BR Black
5310 (26010)	Class 26	Operational	BR Green
31271 *Stratford 1840-2001*	Class 31	Operational	Railfreight Construction
1566 (47449)	Class 47	Operational	BR Blue
Ex-Industrial Diesel Locos			
D2892 *Pilkington* (2782)	Yorkshire 0-4-0	Operational	BR Green
D2899 (2854)	Yorkshire 0-4-0	Undergoing repair	BR Black
Diesel Multiple Units			
50447	Class 104 DMBS	Stored	BR Green
50454	Class 104 DMBS	Operational	BR Blue
50528	Class 104 DMCL	Stored	BR Blue
56456	Class 105 DTCL	Undergoing restoration	BR Green
51933	Class 108 DMBS	Operational	BR Green
54504	Class 108 DTCL	Operational	BR Green
56223	Class 108 DTCL	Operational	BR Green
50416	Class 109 DMBS	Operational	BR Green
56171	Class 109 DTCL	Operational	BR Green
51618	Class 127 DMBS	Undergoing repair	BR Green
Ex-BR Steam Locos			
3802	GWR 2884 Class 2-8-0	Operational	BR Unlined Black
5532	GWR 4575 Class 2-6-2T	Undergoing restoration	GWR Green
7754	GWR 5700 Class Pannier 0-6-0PT	Undergoing overhaul	BR Black
80072	BR Standard 4 2-6-4T	Undergoing overhaul	BR Lined Black
Ex-Industrial Steam Locos			
5459 *Austin 1*	Kitson and Company 0-6-0ST	Operational	Lined Green

On the Llangollen Railway, in open countryside between Glyndfrdwy and Carrog, GWR 4-4-0 3440 *City of Truro* is seen paired with GWR 2-6-2 5526 during the 'Steam, Steel and Stars' steam gala, which took place on 11–26 April 2009.

Pontypool and Blaenavon Railway

The railway, the highest preserved standard-gauge line in the United Kingdom, runs for 2 miles from Whistle Inn Halt to Blaenavon. It features the only standard gauge rail-over-rail bridge within preservation. Opened in 1866, the line was soon absorbed by the LNWR as part of the 'Heads of The Valley' network for coal transportation. Following closure of the through routes in 1941, and finally Big Pit in 1980, the line reopened in 1983, with extensions to Blaenavon High Level in 2010 and Big Pit Halt in 2011.

Getting there: Stagecoach bus service X24 (24 on Sundays) serves Blaenavon High Level station. Ask to alight at Cemetery Bridge, just before Blaenavon Town. By car, free parking at Furnace Sidings station – NP4 9SF, NP4 9AX.

Refreshments: Fireman's Shovel Refreshment Rooms at Furnace Sidings, drinks and snacks only. Pub: Rhymney Brewery Visitor Centre, 25 minutes' walk.

Future plans: There are possible extensions north to Brynmawr and southward to Varteg initially, and, further in the future, to Wainfelin. From Pontypool, restoration of the original route further down the valley is not possible after the construction of the A4043 bypass.

Website: https://www.bhrailway.co.uk

Number(s) (Operating Number Highlighted)	Type	Status	Livery
Ex-BR Diesel Locos			
D5627 *Steve Organ GM* (**31203**)	Class 31	Operational	BR Green
37023	Class 37	Undergoing restoration	BR Large Logo Blue
D6916 (**37216**)	Class 37	Undergoing restoration	BR Green
Ex-Industrial Diesel Locos			
NCB DL16	Hudswell Clarke 0-4-0DH	Stored	Blue
1344	Hudswell Clarke 0-4-0DH	Operational	Blue
170 *Ebbw*	Hunslet 0-8-0DH	Undergoing restoration	Green
5511	Hunslet 0-6-0	Operational	Dark Green
5511	Hunslet 0-6-0DM	Operational	Blue
RT1	John Fowler 0-6-0	Undergoing restoration	Blue
Diesel Multiple Units			
51351	Class 117 DMBS	Undergoing restoration	Primer
51397	Class 117 DMS	Undergoing restoration	BR Green
Ex-BR Steam Locos			
9629	GWR 5700 Class 0-6-0ST	Undergoing restoration	Primer
Ex-Industrial Steam locos			
Rosyth No 1	Andrew Barclay 0-4-0ST	Operational	Green
2201 *Victory*	Andrew Barclay 0-4-0ST	Undergoing restoration	Red
2074 *Llantarnam Abbey*	Andrew Barclay 0-6-0ST	Undergoing restoration	Primer
1515	Hunslet Austerity 0-6-0ST	Awaiting Repairs	Red

Number(s) (Operating Number Highlighted)	Type	Status	Livery
18 *Jessie*	Hunslet 0-6-0ST	Operational	Black
3061 *Empress*	Bagnall 0-6-0ST	Operational	Dark Blue
71515	Avonside Engine Co. 0-6-0ST	Awaiting Restoration	Green
1219 *Caledonia Works*	Andrew Barclay 0-4-0ST	Operational	Green
Swansea Vale No 1 (9622)	Sentinel 0-4-0T	Undergoing restoration	Blue

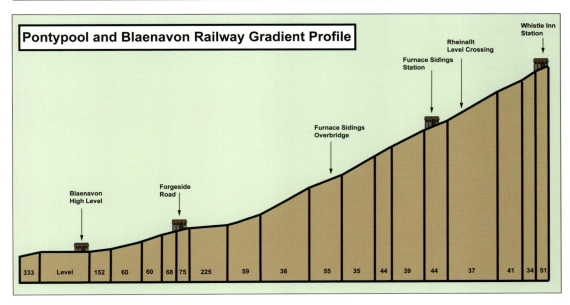

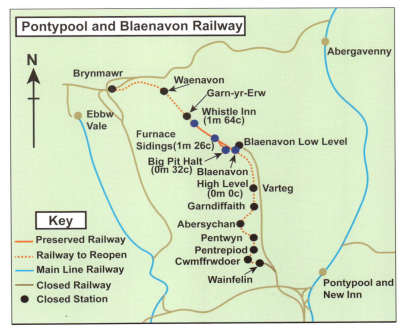

Appendix
Other Preserved Railways

Here is a list of further preserved railways in Britain.

South West
Bideford Railway Heritage Centre: www.bidefordrailway.co.uk
Helston Railway: www.helstonrailway.co.uk
Plym Valley Railway: www.plymrail.co.uk
Somerset & Dorset Railway: sdjr.co.uk
Yeovil Railway Centre: www.yeovilrailway.freeservers.com

South East
Buckinghamshire Railway Centre: www.bucksrailcentre.org
East Kent Railway: eastkentrailway.co.uk
Isle of Wight Steam Railway: iwsteamrailway.co.uk
Lavender Line: www.lavender-line.co.uk
Mail Rail: www.postalmuseum.org/visit-us/what-to-expect/mail-rail
Romney, Hythe & Dymchurch Railway: www.rhdr.org.uk
Rother Valley Railway: www.rvr.org.uk

East of England
Bure Valley Railway: www.bvrw.co.uk
East Anglian Railway Museum: www.earm.co.uk
Leighton Buzzard Railway: www.buzzrail.uk
Mangapps Railway: www.mangapps.co.uk

East Midlands
Lincolnshire Wolds Railway: www.lincolnshirewoldsrailway.co.uk
Northampton Ironstone Railway Trust: www.nir.org.uk
Rocks by Rail: www.rocks-by-rail.org
Rushden, Higham and Wellingborough Railway: rhts.co.uk

West Midlands
Cambrian Heritage Railways: www.cambrianrailways.com
Foxfield Railway: foxfieldrailway.co.uk
Tanat Valley Light Railway: www.tanatvalleyrailway.co.uk
Telford Steam Railway: www.telfordsteamrailway.co.uk

Yorkshire
Derwent Valley Light Railway: dvlr.org.uk
Middleton Railway: www.middletonrailway.org.uk
Yorkshire Wolds Railway: www.yorkshirewoldsrailway.org.uk

North West
Crewe Heritage Centre: www.crewehc.co.uk
Eden Valley Railway: www.evr-cumbria.org.uk
Kirkby Stephen East: www.kirkbystepheneast.co.uk
Ravenglass and Eskdale Railway: ravenglass-railway.co.uk
Ribble Steam Railway and Museum: ribblesteam.org.uk

North East
Aln Valley Railway: www.alnvalleyrailway.co.uk
Darlington Railway Museum/Head of Steam: www.head-of-steam.co.uk
Locomotion: www.locomotion.org.uk
Tanfield Railway: www.tanfield-railway.co.uk

Scotland
Caledonian Railway: caledonianrailway.com
Keith & Dufftown Railway: keith-dufftown-railway.co.uk
Royal Deeside Railway: www.deeside-railway.co.uk
Whitrope Heritage Centre: wrha.org.uk

Wales
Bala Lake Railway: bala-lake-railway.co.uk
Barry Tourist Railway: www.visitthevale.com/attractions/BarryTouristRailway
Brecon Mountain Railway: www.bmr.wales
Corris Railway: www.corris.co.uk
Ffestiniog & Welsh Highland Railways: www.festrail.co.uk
Garw Valley Railway: www.garwvalleyrailway.co.uk
Gwili Railway: gwili-railway.co.uk
Llanberis Lake Railway: www.lake-railway.co.uk
Llanelli & Mynydd Mawr Railway: www.llanellirailway.co.uk
Snowdon Mountain Railway: snowdonrailway.co.uk
Talyllyn Railway: www.talyllyn.co.uk
Welsh Highland Heritage Railway: www.whr.co.uk
Welshpool & Llanfair Light Railway: wllr.org.uk
Vale of Rheidol Railway: www.rheidolrailway.co.uk